# What Others Say About Doug Giles

*"Doug Giles sucks. His books are stoopid. They should be baned and then burnt."*

– Alexandria Haranger

*"Doug Giles is filled with rasicism, sexicism, bigottry and he's drunk on Islamophoria. Plus no one licks him."*

– Joy Knowmoore

*"I don't personally know this Doug Giles guy but I loathe him."*

– Suzy Nabor

*"Knock, knock?*

*Who's there?*

*Doug Giles.*

*Doug Giles who?*

*Exactly."*

– Nancy Isolep

*"Doug Giles says he loves God. But Dougie boy doesn't know that God is a fairy-tale and I hate him."*

– Crispin Little Flower


*"Lets see: Doug identifies as a White, Christian, Straight, Male. In other words Doug's everything thing that are wrong with THE WHOLE PLANET!"*

– Greta Coldgurl


*"John the Baptist never existed. Doug Giles should have never existed. It's that simple"*

– Katy Due

Published by White Feather Press. (www.whitefeatherpress.com)
Edited by Karen Walker.
ISBN 978-1-61808-215-2
Printed in the United States of America
Cover design by David Bugnon and mobopolis.com

Dedication

This quick read is for all my prophetic brothers and sisters out there in evangelical la-la-land. You are needed now more than ever. Pick up your whip and start clearing the punks.

# John The Baptist

## A Rude Awakening Precedes
## A Great Awakening

# By Doug Giles

Table of Contents

## About the Art

The art work contained in these pages was painted by yours truly. Some originals, herein, are still available. All of these images are available as Open Edition Prints that can be customized to fit your wall space. We print on museum quality canvas, luster paper, wood and for all you metal-heads, we also print on metal. We use only the best inks in our printing process. To see these pieces and more go to Doug-Giles.Art.

# Introduction

Because I regularly paint, write, podcast, and preach about the various fascinating folks in the Bible I often get asked, "who's my favorite character in the scripture?" To wit, I reply … uh … that would be Jesus. What kind of goofy question is that? He's my Lord and Savior. He's my Rock, my Rescuer, my Restorer, my Redeemer, my Protector, my Provider, my Friend, my Brother, Yea, He's the King of Kings and the Lord of Lords. So … yeah … I kind of like Him a little bit more than others. Hello.

That said, I do have many eccentric critters that I have taken a shinin' to via the *Verbum Dei*.

For instance, I love Peter. He's the disciple with the foot-shaped mouth. He's the one who was a tad slow on the spiritual uptick, if you know what I mean. He's the one who cussed a blue cloud when he blew it badly. He's the sword-wielding disciple that'll cut yo' dang head off for Christ. Ol' Pete had the capacity to speak divine revelation in one moment and be the mouthpiece for Satan seven verses later (Mt. 16:16,23). Indeed, Pedro's the one that I can look to that God greatly used in spite of all his glaring inconsistencies. Inconsistencies that, unfortunately, I, too, sport in spades. Help me, Lord! Help me.

King David is also a favorite of mine for many of the same reasons Peter is. He was a very flawed dude who had a heart after God and triumphantly kicked backside on his personal demons and his physical enemies. Hoorah.

My list could go on and on about the summit-or-plummet saints that lived a truly storied life for the Kingdom of God. Men and women who weren't just quaint little Christians, but hell-robbers, hell-razers, and earthshakers. They were men and women who upset the world (Acts 17:6). The writer of Hebrews' homage to these amazing humans says it way better than this public schoolie ever could. Check it out...

> *And what more shall I say? For time will fail me if I tell of Gideon, Barak, Samson, Jephthah, of David and Samuel and the prophets, who by faith conquered kingdoms, performed acts of righteousness, obtained promises, shut the mouths of lions, quenched the power of fire, escaped the edge of the sword, from weakness were made strong, became mighty in war, put foreign armies to flight. Women received back their dead by resurrection; and others were tortured, not accepting their release, so that they might obtain a better resurrection; and others experienced mocking and flogging, and further, chains and imprisonment. They were stoned, they were sawn in two, they were tempted, they were put to death with the sword; they went about in sheepskins, in goatskins, being destitute, afflicted, tormented (people of whom the world was not worthy), wandering in deserts, on mountains, and sheltering in caves and holes in the ground.*
>
> – Heb. 11:32-38 (NASB)

People of whom the world was not worthy?

Wow.

What an accolade.

By the way, that bravo was given by the Holy Ghost who inspired the writer of Hebrews to jot that down for all eternity. Wouldn't it be wonderful if we got that type of kudos from the Godhead once we took the big dirt nap? I think it would be.

There is one person that is absent from that list, who also knew God and did exploits and that person is … drum roll please … John the Baptist. Or John, the Reformed Presbyterian, as I like to call him. John the Baptist was a fascinating cat, to say the least. He's been the subject of several of my oil paintings. I hope to God there is some way to watch videos in heaven because I would love to see John the Baptist preach and compare his message, delivery, and stalwartness to the tinkerpots that are currently occupying pulpits in our effete, and-oh-so-sassy, evangelical world of popinjays.

I think the church in America needs at least 100,000 John the Baptists as soon as possible.

A lot of the Church is sick, folks. It's anemic.

We've become wussies for Christ, instead of warriors for Christ.

Whole slices of Christendom became obedient to various Faucis and big government goons from 2020-2022 and shut down their churches lest they be fined. John the Baptist and the other prophets and apostles would've never shut their churches down like a lot of pusillanimous pastors did.

Shameful.

By the way, if your pastor did shut his church down

and did do all the other ridiculous junk the government told him to, have they publicly repented for being a coward (Rev. 21:8, Acts 5:39) and kissing Mayor McCheese's glutes for the last couple of years?

Chunks of the church have become woke to anti-biblical *bovine scatology*, sported by anti-theistic Marxists, that Christ, the apostles, and the prophets wouldn't have stomached for one nanosecond.

In addition to that sad slop, the pulpit has been gooeyfied with toothless psychobabble sermons that have ill-equipped God's people to stand and fight in the evil day (Eph. 5:16, Eph. 6:13). This little offering you're reading right now attempts to rectify that ridiculous and unholy footing.

Herewith are my fourteen reasons why we need more men in the pulpit like John the Baptist instead of sweet little choir boys who are scared of their own shadows.


Doug Giles
April 1st, 2023.
Somewhere in Texas

(*You can find my renditions of John the Baptist online at DougGiles.Art in my Biblical Badass Gallery. We have prints of them all and a few originals still available.)

# Chapter One: Of Puppets and Prophets

A puppet can mimic a human, an animal, some alien critter, or a character ripped from the pages of mythology.

When my daughters were little, my wife and I bought them a rubber frog and a rubber piglet hand puppet. They were super cheap gifts that provided mega amounts of entertainment. Especially after I had a couple of beers.

Puppets come in all shapes and sizes. You've got your entry-level, economic, finger and sock puppets. Then you've got the advanced-level Marionette, which is way more difficult to navigate, as it is suspended and controlled by a sick number of strings that's too complicated for this redneck's attention span, skillset, and interest.

Then there's your rod puppets that are controlled by a rod that's attached to a head. In addition, we also have shadow puppets which are cut-out figures held between a light source and a see-through screen.

And lastly, we have the ventriloquist's dummy. This puppet is operated by the ventriloquist's hand while producing the puppet's voice with *muy poquito* mouth movements on the puppeteer's behalf. This creates an illusion that the puppet is alive and yapping.

My favorite ventriloquist is Jeff Dunham. That dude's a trip and his various puppet characters are a scream. I was watching him last night and I laughed so hard that milk came out of my nostrils, and I haven't had milk since 1986.

Although varied in their shapes, sizes, and operational systems the one thing all puppets have in common is: they are manipulated by a puppeteer. Yep, it's the puppeteer's voice and actions you're hearing and seeing, not the puppets. Ergo, everything that appears to be tumbling out of Tumbalina's fake mouth is coming from the puppet master's piehole.

The scriptures are replete with examples of false prophets and priests who were mere puppets of some human and/or demonic religious machine while pretending to be spokespersons for God.

John the Baptist was no puppet. He was a prophet. Jesus even said He was *more* than a prophet (Mt. 11:9). John the Baptist was a voice, not an echo. He left holy scars on the souls of those who were fortunate enough to have heard him preach.

Nowadays, we have all kinds of puppets in the pulpits. We have Politically Correct Puppets in pulpits. Yea, we have veritable Woke Puppets in pulpits today parroting what this putrid culture peddles.

In addition, we have Big Government Puppet Pastors who take their marching orders from civil magistrates versus the Lord Jesus Christ.

Good Lawd! I almost forgot. The church also has I Love Money Puppets in pulpits, as well as the ubiquitous Ear-tickling Puppets who preside over America's Evangelical Enterprise. Cha-ching!

As you're about to read, John the Baptist didn't play those stupid, sad, sinful, and satanic games with God, God's word, and God's call on his life.

Oh, no *senorita.*

John the Baptist was straight up in his motivation and his message and that's why John is appealing and most modern ministers are appalling. Unlike the various puppets, John the Baptist was unmanipulatable by pressures to conform or be canceled. The only one who could move John's mouth was the Lord God Almighty. John feared no man. Can that be said about you? Or are you a puppet of appeasement and compromise?

# John The Baptist

# Chapter Two: You Can't Have Jesus Without John

*John the Baptist appeared in the wilderness, preaching a baptism of repentance for the forgiveness of sins... John was clothed with camel's hair and wore a leather belt around his waist, and his diet was locusts and wild honey. And he was preaching, saying, "After me One is coming who is mightier than I, and I am not fit to bend down and untie the straps of His sandals. I baptized you with water; but He will baptize you with the Holy Spirit."*

— Mark 1:4-8 (NASB)

Question: If you were going to pick someone to be the forerunner for the most important human being and human event to ever grace this planet; I'm talking about the dude who was to introduce

Jesus to the world and assist Him in kicking off His earthly ministry, whom would you pick to introduce Him?

Would you choose an angel? Howzabout Gabriel with his trumpet? That would be a cool and stunning intro for Immanuel, eh?

Oh, wait! What about another virgin, like Mary? Say, some girl from Puerto Rico to give our team a bit more of an inclusionary and international flair?

Or ... or ... maybe we could tap a "dignified" Christian statesman like Mike Pence for the gig. What do you think? He'd give the event a bit of gray-headed gravitas, correct?

I know. We should appoint some hip Christian actress like Candace Cameron Bure to chair the ceremony. Or maybe Kathie Lee Gifford. She'd be a good emcee with her fresh Balance of Nature va-va-voom vibe.

Dang it. I almost forgot. What if we got a cool, trendy, patchouli-scented, young hipster dude, who is over-ebullient and does effective and manipulative voice inflections while he preaches his smooth sermons on Sunday?

One thing is for certain: I guarantee our neutered churches and our squeamish pastoral search committees would not have picked John the Baptist.

Oh. Heck. No.

John was too terse. Too austere. Too unconventional. Too unbeholden, too unimpressed, and too unbowed. Frilly religious peeps can't control a man like that who's not into their badinage about bourgeois religious crap. Ergo, they wouldn't have chosen him.

Plus, John the Baptist wore strange clothes, rebuked esteemed leaders to their faces, had no formal education, lived in the wild, ate grasshoppers, was cuddly as a cactus, and his pulpit was a muddy creek.

John, you see, would not be Google-friendly. ReputationDefender.com would definitely red-flag his online presence.

Indeed, dearly beloved, the timid, tamed, and tepid wouldn't touch John's ministry with a ten-foot pew. Here's why …

John the Baptist was a holy wildman that came off more like Ronnie James Dio than Joel Osteen. What is dangerous about the wildman is he is a nightmare to cultural, political, and ecclesiastical arrangements that keep men in a state of craven compliance or enculturated as obedient stooges of the machine.

John was liberated from that noise. He was bold, wild, and free from those authoritarian pressures to conform. This wildman had perfected holy defiance. Rebellion to tyrants was John's obedience to God.

John wasn't impressed by what other religious leaders held in high esteem. As you will see later on in this slim opus, He couldn't be cowed by the siren sounds of political or ecclesiastical correctness, or threats of imprisonment or death.

He was holy, implacable, and secure in his peculiar

role. He was smitten only with the approval of God.

Jesus, obviously, in His incarnation, dug him. Matter of fact, Jesus said of those born among women, there are none ... like in zero, zilch, nada, no one greater than John. Not Abraham, Isaac, Jacob, Joseph, Moses, Joshua, nor any of the Judges; or King David, Elijah, Elisha, Solomon, or any of the major or minor prophets. No one. John the Baptist bested them all, at that juncture, according to Christ.

The interesting thing about John the Baptist was that he had nothing that the others sported in spades. No miracles. No formal education. No riches. He was born to a couple of old geezers. He was sent to school where there was no school, just earth, wind, and fire ... and God, of course. His ministry was molded during three decades of isolation.

Oh, by the way, John prepared thirty years for an amazing ministry that lasted just a few years. Ministers today prepare just a couple of years for a milquetoast ministry that lasts thirty years.

Most blind guides today would say, "Nope, we'll pass on John to introduce sweet Jesus to the planet, thank you very much."

However, for the Father, Son, and the Holy Spirit, John the Baptist was the perfect person to go before Jesus the Son, and get the crowd's attention that stuff's about to abruptly change. And please note: God did it through a wildman with a turn-or-burn message. The coming of Jesus was accompanied by the person and the work of John the Baptist.

# John The Baptist

If you want "Jesus" in your life, church, culture, or nation, you'd better brace your soul for a "John the Baptist" because according to Malachi 4:5, you can't have one without the other.

John was a wrecking ball to business-as-usual Churchianity.

He was preparing the way for the Master, therefore he had to flatten many sacred cows. And people *loved* their sacred cows.

Pardon my redundancy, but the politically incorrect ministry of John the Baptist was the prelude to the person and work of Jesus Christ. John was the opening act. If we want "Jesus" in our life, home, family, church, and culture then we must brace ourselves for "John's" abrasive message of repentance.

In addition, do not think the vehicle delivering this message of repentance is going to be palatable to the persnickety religious person's penchants. God usually uses the base and corrupt to confront the haughty and smarmy. If you don't believe me, Google 1Cor. 1:26-31.

The message that will eternally change you, will first immediately offend you. The messenger, like John, will offend you as well. Those who hunger and thirst for righteousness are cool with both. They don't care if their flesh gets pinched and the message gets pitched by a wild prophet. All they want is God's will to be done, on earth as it is in heaven.

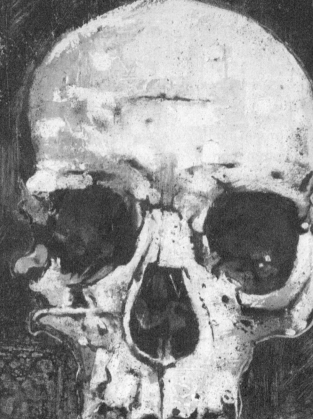

JUDGMENT

COMETH

# Chapter Three:
# In Your Face

C heck out Mark's introduction of John the Baptist
...

*The beginning of the gospel of Jesus Christ,*
*the Son of God; As it is written in the prophets,*
*Behold, I send my messenger before thy face,*
*which shall prepare thy way before thee. The*
*voice of one crying in the wilderness, Prepare*
*ye the way of the Lord, make his paths straight.*
*John did baptize in the wilderness, and preach*
*the baptism of repentance for the remission of*
*sins. And there went out unto him all the land*
*of Judaea, and they of Jerusalem, and were*
*all baptized of him in the river of Jordan, con-*
*fessing their sins. And John was clothed with*
*camel's hair, and with a girdle of a skin about*
*his loins; and he did eat locusts and wild honey;*
*And preached, saying, There cometh one might-*
*ier than I after me, the latchet of whose shoes I*

*am not worthy to stoop down and unloose.*

*I indeed have baptized you with water: but he shall baptize you with the Holy Ghost.*

*– Mark 1:1-8 (KJV)*

Here are three observations regarding John from the prior eight passages. Are you ready? Good. Let's giddy up.

**Point Number One:** *"As it is written in the prophets, Behold, I send my messenger before thy face, which shall prepare thy way before thee." –* Mk. 1:2 (KJV)

Mark's grounding John the Baptist's presence and preaching in the prophets (Isaiah & Malachi). John's message was not a product of some jacked-up clueless culture. John wasn't an amalgam created in a Bible School laboratory to make Jesus groovy to godless goobers. Also, please note that John's not quoting Oprah, *The View,* or CNN. John's ministry is biblically based. It's grounded in the prophets. His ministry was foretold and fulfilled. This is otherworldly stuff, y'all. This is not some preaching gig that John took up because he failed as an *American Idol* hopeful and has to make some cash somehow. This unique man was the fulfillment of ancient prophecy. John's ministry has God all over it. Again, I must ask you to pardon my redundancy, but very few carnal-to-the-core elder boards would've chosen a wild critter like John, but God did. Indeed, that obtuse character, named John the Baptist, was supernaturally crafted to purposely run afoul with the self-righteous as a waymaker for the Son of God. I so love the fact that God chooses and greatly uses folks that most religious do-gooders would throw rotten eggs at.

Make certain, preacher, that your ministry is biblically-based and you're not glomming onto some bollocks our sullied society is swilling. So, exactly what am I saying here? Well, it is simple, my brethren. It is this: Be like John the Baptist and not Justin the Bieber.

**Point Number Two:** *"Behold, I send my messenger before thy face, which shall prepare thy way before thee."* – Mk.1:2b (KJV)

If John the Baptist's ministry was anything, it was an "in your face" ministry. It was not a cute ministry. Or a friendly ministry. Or a Tony Robbins-like ministry with a Christian flair. John's ministry was "before thy face". It was confrontational, y'all. It would be considered crass if your heart happened to be hardened to God and spot-welded to external religious rules and regulations. Yep, if that was you then Ol' Johnny would be loathsome in your eyes because he didn't play your pompous games. Not only did John not play religious games but he jet-blasted those who did, in public, with some of the most delicious and scathing rebukes. Here's a tasty sample …

> *When John realized that a lot of Pharisees and Sadducees were showing up for a baptismal experience because it was becoming the popular thing to do, he exploded: "Brood of snakes! What do you think you're doing slithering down here to the river? Do you think a little water on your snakeskins is going to make any difference? It's your life that must change, not your skin! And don't think you can pull rank by claiming Abraham as father.*

*Being a descendant of Abraham is neither here nor there. Descendants of Abraham are a dime a dozen. What counts is your life. Is it green and flourishing? Because if it's dead-wood, it goes on the fire.*

– Mt. 3:7-10 (TM)

When's the last time you heard a pastor pop off like that? John called the high and mighty religious leaders snakes to their faces and in front of a big stonkin' crowd of truth-seeking peeps.

And you know what?

That was just what God ordered. That was a Divine thing. God ordained and inspired John the Baptist to let those religious fat cats have it right between the eyes in front of everyone and their camel. John's message and delivery were not subtle and safely nuanced to land easily on the listener's delicate psyche. This brutal, con-frontational, admin of God's word was the prelude to the earthly ministry of the Son of God.

So, what's my point? Well, for this little nugget, it is this: as long as pastors continue to be nicer-than-Christ don't expect Jesus to show up in a true and profound way. Yep, if you don't have an "in your face" edge to your ministry then bad religion will flourish and the True Jesus won't be anywhere near your "church".

Remember, the rough and tumble ministry of John was inextricably linked to the ministry of Jesus. You can't have one without the other.

**Point Number Three:** *"John did baptize in the wilder-ness, and preach the baptism of repentance for the re-*

*mission of sins. And there went out unto him all the land of Judaea, and they of Jerusalem, and were all baptized of him in the river of Jordan, confessing their sins."*

- Mk. 1:4-5 (KJV)

Dear Church: "Preparing the way for Jesus", equated a message of repentance and a confession of sin/sins.

Confession of sin? Who does that anymore?

Repentance? Yeah, right.

Those are two little ditties you don't hear much about in church now, do you?

Nah, it's just blather like ...

- God has a wonderful plan for your life.

- Just ask sweet Jesus into your heart.

- Jesus is outside the door of your heart. He's cold and He's knocking on your door. Won't you please let Him in before He catches pneumonia?

- Jesus wants you to realize your full potential and live your best life now.

To wit, I say, WTH?

That's not what John and Jesus preached. They preached repentance and the people confessed and dumped their sins and followed Christ fully.

Speaking of sin, when's the last time you heard a message that painted the unrepentant sinner as damned, condemned to an eternal hell, and outside of Christ? That their only remedy was to do a 180 from that wayward path of willful wickedness and trust wholly in Christ alone?

What's that I hear? Is that crickets? I thought so.

Sin's not a big whoop anymore. We don't even call sin, *sin*. We've defined deviancy down. Now it's a problem, or an addiction, or an alternative lifestyle, or a disorder, or not the greatest path one could choose. Paul said sin is rebellion that brings on the wrath of God and that there is no little sin, because there is no little God to sin against (Rom. 1:18).

Seldom have I seen a big demonstration of sorrow for sins committed but I do see it, as in big time, within the Old Testament and the New.

In Ezra 9:3, when Ezra saw the people of God marrying gentile pirate hookers, Ezra was so disturbed by this unclean covenant violation that he pulled out his own hair and beard. And get this: he didn't even commit that sin but repented of it on their impenitent behalf. Now, *that's* what you call a confession of sin. Ripping your beard out you're so disgusted with bad behavior. Churches nowadays wouldn't be yanking their bohemian beards out if some Church dude married a kookie Kardashian-type of chick. On the contrary, we'd probably throw them a dance party complete with a Billie Eilish cover band and some taco food trucks. Not so with Ezra. He knew full well that Israel had grievously sinned and that was bad news bears for the people of God.

Where true conversion occurred, via the scripture, it

entailed stuff like …

- Men and women tearing their clothes (Jer. 36:24).

- Shaving one's head (Job. 1:20).

- When Isaiah saw God he said, "Woe is me. I'm ruined" (Isa. 6:5).

- Paul called his flesh wretched … a body of death (Rom. 7:14-25).

Nowadays, in church, that kind of confession is weird. Sadly, that type of drastic reaction and massive life change is the exception, not the rule, in today's Church of the Warm & Fuzzies.

Currently, it's like, "how many wanna accept Cool Jesus who doesn't expect you to quit your rebellion against God?" That's pretty much the unspoken message. Sorry, I was wrong. That *is* the spoken message false prophets are giving to the Tickle-My-Ear masses.

So, biblically speaking, what is true repentance? What does it look like? How do we know if we have truly repented from whatever it is we're practicing?

Well, to answer that question we gotta go to the Bible, correct?

Check out the Apostle Paul's definition of what it means to genuinely repent.

*For though I caused you sorrow by my letter, I do not regret it; though I did regret it—for I see that that letter caused you sorrow, though only for a while— I now rejoice, not that you were made sorrowful, but that you were made sorrow-ful to the point of repentance; for you were made sorrowful according to the will of God, so that you might not suffer loss in anything through us. For the sorrow that is according to the will of God produces a repentance without regret, leading to salvation, but the sorrow of the world produces death. For behold what earnestness this very thing, this godly sorrow, has produced in you: what vindication of yourselves, what indignation, what fear, what longing, what zeal, what punishment of wrong! In everything you demonstrated yourselves to be innocent in the matter.. – 2 Cor. 7:8-11 (NASB)*

Lemme break it down for you. Here we go...

1. Repentance entails grief and pain. Yes, little children. God'll make you feel like crap and send pain when we're out of sorts with Him. Check out John 16:8 if you don't believe me.

2. The grief and pain God allows is profitable. It turns you back to God. It leads to a deliverance from evil and that is *bueno*, amen?

3. True repentance makes you eager and earnest to run away from filth.

4. True repentance removes blame and suspicion of wrongdoing.

5. True repentance makes you indignant regarding the sinful things you once enjoyed.

6. True repentance produces the fear of God.

7. True repentance produces a longing for the Lord.

8. True repentance produces a holy zeal for the things of God.

9. True repentance makes one punish what's bogus in their life.

10. True repentance removes guilt from the guilty party.

As stated, John's message was repent. He preached that message unashamedly and in the folks' faces. And you know what? The ones who were broken and hungry for the Lord loved the message of repentance and the ones who were stuck in their self-righteous ways did not and they all went to hell for their stubborn religious rebellion.

# Chapter Four: John Was Not a Glory Boy

*And (John) preached, saying, There cometh one mightier than I after me, the latchet of whose shoes I am not worthy to stoop down and unloose.*

*— Mark 1:7 (KJV)*

Check out how these other translations render the above text …

John also told the people, *"Someone more powerful is going to come. And I am not good enough even to stoop down and untie his sandals."* (CEV)

Here is a sample of his preaching: *"Someone is coming soon who is far greater than I am, so much greater that I am not even worthy to be his slave."* (TLB)

*"Someone a lot stronger than me is coming close behind,' John used to tell them. 'I don't deserve to squat down and undo his sandals."* (NTE)

"I'm not good enough?"

"I'm not even worthy to be His slave?"

"I don't deserve to squat down and undo his sandals?"

Who the heck says that any more?

The body of Christ, especially in the American milieu, sounds more like Stuart Smalley instead of John the Baptist. Most believers are like, "I'm good enough. I'm smart enough. And gosh darn it ... people like me." Not John. John knew in the historical scheme of redemptive history he was an important, stonkin', legitimate, biblical badass. Yet, compared to Christ ... eh ... he was a pipsqueak and he knew it.

I'm not into groveling before God, and I don't think John was groveling at all when he said he was not worthy to untie Jesus' shoes. What I dig about John's assessment of his importance versus Jesus' eminence was John knew that true ministry is about Jesus and not one's self.

Ministry today is all about me, me, me, and me! We're Salvation egoists. Mere, self-obsessed, religious me-monkeys. Yes indeed, we are a gaggle of solipsistic navel-gazers who make Narcissus look like a self-loathing, penitent monk.

# John The Baptist

Nowadays, you're made to feel bad as a minister if you're not a Fox News contributor, if you're not on Christian TV and/or if you don't have at least a million followers on Facebook, and you should especially feel weird if you still fly coach! We're told … "you're not blessed if you're not a social media influencer at the highest level."

John was just the opposite of today's self-preening peacocks. John wanted his "brand" to diminish and Jesus's "brand" to catch fire. Again, who in ministry does that any more?

One of my favorite authors is a man named T. Austin-Sparks (1888-1971). TAS is one of the most brilliant, deep divers, of the person and work of Christ that I've ever had the privilege to read. One of the stories I heard about him from David Wilkerson was that, as a minister, Austin-Sparks hated publicity. He hated having his picture taken. He loathed the glamor/ PR-sizzle when it came to preaching. I have a stack of his books and not one of them has his mugshot on them. I didn't even know what he looked like after reading his works for the last thirty-five years until I Googled him a few months ago. TAS was more concerned with folks closing in with Christ than you admiring his biceps, his Armani Exchange polo shirt, his tattoos, his way-too-skinny jeans, and his fresh *Peaky Blinders* hairdo. I'm a guessin' that TAS and John the Baptist would've gotten along swimmingly if they were contemporaries.

In John the Baptist's last testimony of Christ, he's still singing the same song as he did when he launched his epic forerunner, demon-thrashing ministry: namely … it ain't about me and it's all about Him. Check it out …

> *Then a matter of dispute developed on the part of John's disciples with a Jew about purification. And they came to John and said to him, "Rabbi, He who was with you beyond the Jordan, to whom you have testified—behold, He is baptizing and all the people are coming to Him." John replied, "A person can receive not even one thing unless it has been given to him from heaven. You yourselves are my witnesses that I said, 'I am not the Christ,' but, 'I have been sent ahead of Him.' He who has the bride is the groom; but the friend of the groom, who stands and listens to him, rejoices greatly because of the groom's voice. So this joy of mine has been made full. He must increase, but I must decrease.*

> – Jn. 3:25-30 (NASB)

John's disciples seem ticked off that Jesus is baptizing more people than John. In other words, they're just like ministers today who're caught up in nickles, noses, and numbers versus Christ. John's like, "Yo' dudes … that's what is supposed to happen. He is supposed to be the VIP and I am supposed to fade from the stage. Is there something wrong with your hearing? That's what I have been thundering ever since the get-go" (Author's paraphrase).

# John The Baptist

John was joyful that his ministry was decreasing and Jesus' ministry was increasing? That's cuckoo talk into today's mephitic culture of ministerial self-importance. When's the last time you heard a preacher say, "I wanna be less important?" Or, "Y'know what? I need to become less and less?" Or … "I think I need to slip off to the sidelines?" John not only said it, he did it. John, you see, was no glory boy.

# Chapter Five: All Hell Breaks Loose

*From the days of John the Baptist until now the kingdom of heaven suffers violence, and violent men take it by force.*

– Matthew 11:12 (NASB)

The preceding text is one you'll never hear preached at your typical youth group.

In addition, you'll probably never hear a minister use that verse to set the mood for their Church's New Years' Resolutions.

Why do pastors avoid this epic text?

Well, it's too terse and too obtuse for the soft-focus, bearded lady, *faux* Jesus they've been foisting on their easily offended and self-deceived crowd and if they run them off, they won't be able to afford their mistress's Mercedes any longer.

So, *ipso facto*, this verse gets passed over like low-fat yogurt does at a plus-sized nacho party.

If you think I'm exaggerating about the extreme neglect of this important admonition from the Son of Man by most ministers nowadays, then take this simple test: Go to your church's sermon archives and do a Matthew 11:12 word search and see if it pops up. Good luck.

So, let's dig into this little biblical nugget, shall we?

Jesus said, *"From the days of John the Baptist until now the kingdom of heaven suffers violence, and violent men take it by force."*

When John the Baptist rocked up on the scene, as the emcee of history's main event, he was a holy wrecking crane to dead religion and evil politicians.

For four hundred-plus years, there was no prophetic word going forth after Malachi's ministry.

God wasn't saying squat. Religion flourished, but God was not speaking. Which is interesting, eh? Four hundred years of deafening silence from Jehovah.

Until John the Baptist.

# John The Baptist

When John opened his mouth he shook all of hell which had been playing peacefully for four centuries.

When John parted his prophetic lips and jet-blasted cocky demons and evil men it was game on, *mamac-ita*.

John was a rowdy, equal opportunity offender and boy howdy ... was John good at his job.

Here's a sidebar: You know what's disgusting?

Have you ever seen how the "Church" has historically depicted John the Baptist in their paintings? Just like Jesus, they have made John look like a bearded woman. Kind of like Mona Lisa's identical, very effeminate, twin brother. Or, for a more timely example, sort of akin to Kate Hudson from *Almost Famous*. If you think I'm full specious doo, google "Leonardo Da Vinci - John the Baptist".

I countered Christendom's epicene art with my own versions of John in my oil painting series I've dubbed, The Biblical Badass Series. You can check it out via DougGiles.Art. I also did a short film around my findings that you can view there as well.

John, like Jesus, was not some little twinkie.

When John preached, you wouldn't go to sleep while he spoke.

When John preached, you wouldn't wonder what he meant.

John branded his listeners' souls.

John spawned conflict everywhere he went.

Where John trod, he left a combination of riots and revival in his wake.

Yep, John generated nothing but solid angst and/or joy when he preached.

That first-century *amigo*, with his call to repentance, stirred up devils in every corridor of hell to such an extent that the only way to shut him down was to cut off his head.

And that's exactly what they did.

Jesus, in light of John's hell-razing ministry, said in effect, if you want to get in on what God's doing now, you're going to have to get and stay spiritually scrappy.

The Kingdom of God brings conflict, and unless we're spiritually violent, we're going to be roadkill under the wheels of satanic attacks.

John and Jesus were verbally attacked, physically assaulted, and both were ultimately murdered for the Message.

Half-hearted commitments to Christ won't suffice ever since John opened up his glorious mouth and let the devils have it.

# John The Baptist

The Amplified Bible puts it this way ...

*And from the days of John the Baptist until the present time, the kingdom of heaven has endured violent assault, and violent men seize it by force (as a precious prize—a share in the heavenly kingdom is sought with most ardent zeal and intense exertion).*

*− Mt. 11:12 (AMP)*

Did you catch what Jesus said was the violent attitude needed for one to "share in the heavenly kingdom?" You have to see being on Jesus' team as a "precious prize" that requires a "most ardent zeal" and "intense exertion". And there went 90% of folks who claim Christ.

Question: How many Christians can you name who value Jesus and His kingdom as a "precious prize?" Not precious in the, "aww isn't that cute" sense of the word, but that which is highly valuable and is esteemed above every other person or thing or aspiration this planet has to offer?

Paul valued the person and work of Christ like that. Check it out in Philippians 3:7,8 (NASB).

*But whatever things were gain to me, these things I have counted as loss because of Christ. More than that, I count all things to be loss in view of the surpassing value of knowing Christ Jesus my Lord, for whom I have suffered the loss of all things, and count them mere rubbish, so that I may gain Christ,*
*...*

Paul's affections ran hot for God. He did violence to everything that tried to seduce him away from the Father and His will. Yep, whether it was his lower cortex, me-monkey, carnal appetites, or his self-righteous religious pedigree, anything that would tempt him away from Christ and Christ alone got the Pauline wood chipper.

Question number two: How many Christian folks do you know who sport a "most ardent zeal" and 'intense exertion?' Who can be characterized as having an extreme, passionate, energetic pursuit of the things of God that is unrelenting in force, degree, and strength in their love and loyalty to Jesus and the Gospel?

This is what Jesus calls, "violence". The people who have these traits are the ones who get "a share in His heavenly kingdom" ever since John opened his holy mouth two thousand years ago.

Make us "violent", Lord.

# Chapter Six: John Goes Medieval on the Pharisees & Sadducees

*But when he (John) saw many of the Pharisees and Sadducees coming for baptism, he said to them, "You offspring of vipers, who warned you to flee from the wrath to come? Therefore produce fruit consistent with repentance; and do not assume that you can say to yourselves, 'We have Abraham as our father'; for I tell you that God is able, from these stones, to raise up children for Abraham. And the axe is already laid at the root of the trees; therefore, every tree that does not bear good fruit is being cut down and thrown into the fire.*

*– Matthew 3:7-10 (NASB)*

Good Lawd! What a rebuke!

I would love to have watched that dress down, wouldn't you? You do know that Jesus was in the crowd when John unleashed that can of whoop-ass on the religious glitterati, right? I bet Christ was having a good laugh as He watched Juan make a Filet-O-Fish sandwich out of these fastidious, uber-religious, self-congratulatory, and self-righteous dandies.

Check it out: John's got the *creme de la creme* of the religious class coming to him to get baptized and he calls them snakes and tells them they are, effectively, on Bon Scott's *Highway to Hell*.

High five, John. High five.

Who does that anymore?

Short answer: not too many ministers.

Why not? Well, it's because they're nicer than John and Jesus.

Most unmanly pastors who love to be loved, need to be needed, and want to be wanted, would be giddy if religious VIPs rocked up to their baptismal services. They'd give them green room access, front row seating, UberLux services to the airport, and splurge for a killer brunch with them after the watery sacrament concluded. They would count themselves "privileged" to be considered worthy of their time and attendance. Not John. He told them to sod off and he did it in front of everyone. That's what you call, "ballsy", my beloved.

To give you a sense of whom John just told to go pound sand, allow yours truly to do a composite sketch of the two groups that JB just BBQ'ed.

Here we go ...

First up to bat are ... The Pharisees.

The Pharisees, which means "separate ones", wanted to please God. But in their attempts to do so, they separated from anyone or anything that their traditions or their misinterpretation of the Law might deem nasty.

The Pharisees developed a contemptuous view of others. They thought they were above certain people's levels of depravity and thus became proud about what they eschewed and what they had achieved. As one minister aptly stated, "Along with their contemptuous view of others, the Pharisees had a shallow sense of forgiveness, a wrong sense of grace and fairness, and an unhealthy view of people's failures."

The Pharisees held to the letter of the Law but were blind to the Spirit of the Law and they had no idea how far off base they were. They separated themselves from environments and people to become pleasing in God's sight – at least that was their intention. This misinterpretation of what the Word said led them to become (hello) the very ones whom God detested.

Oh, by the way, the Pharisees memorized the first five books of the Bible, fasted one week out of every month, had a high view of scripture, paid a tenth to the temple service of everything that they had, and were politically conservative. Sound familiar?

The Pharisees' self-righteous pursuit of outward piety failed to deal with their inward sins of bigotry, rage, envy, pride, love of money, bullying, trap-setting, character assassinations, word games, and death plots. And they did all the aforementioned "all in the name of God". Charming, eh? They fulfilled what St. Paul said: they *"professed to know God, (but) were detestable, disobedient and unfit for any good deed."*

Regarding the second group that got drop-kicked by John namely, the Sadducees, they weren't as religiously persnickety as the Pharisees were. For instance, they denied the resurrection of the dead (Mt .22:23; Mk. 12:18-27; Acts 23:8). They denied miracles. They denied the afterlife, angels, and demons (Acts 23:8) and that's why they were *sad, you see?* Their "faith" was more of a political thang that carved out for them a nice place of power amongst the ruling class. Anything going down in the Temple, or via Roman rule, or in other places of authority, one could always find a Sadducee there kissing butt, or throwing elbows for pole positions. They were the power-hungry DC-type of folks who took on a bare minimum of religious semblance in order to get invited to the fancy meetings with the Who's Who crowds.

Here's an interesting factoid: The Sadducees ceased to exist as a group in AD 70 when Jerusalem and the temple were destroyed by the Romans.

# John The Baptist

So, what do we have here, little children? Well, we have two powerful sects: one that worships their man-made rules versus God and the other that dons religious duds for political gain. With the twain, God was not well pleased. So, the Lord did what a truly loving God should do: He unleashed his holy pitbull, named John the Baptist, to chew on their backside and chew John did.

First off, John calls them an "offspring of vipers." In our parlance, down here in the great Republic of Texas, we'd call them "a rattlesnakes den." For the simpleton who might be reading right now, that is *not* a compliment and that *sobriquet* is rich with biblical meaning. Serpents in the scripture are seen as evil critters, filled with deadly poison, and are linked to the Serpent, also known as the Devil (Gen .3).

Can you imagine these upper-crust, my poop don't stink, oily, religious do-gooder groups that have propped themselves up for the last couple of centuries getting massive insulting shade thrown onto them by a literal Johnny-Come-Lately wildman whose pulpit is a creek? John gave them a nickname they didn't dig: a *brood of vipers*. Oh, by the way, that moniker John labeled the Pharisees with was inspired by the Holy Ghost.

Here's some Bible trivia.

Question: Who also, in the Bible, called the most powerful religious group "a brood of vipers"? Was it …

A. Peter, Paul, John, and Ringo?

B. Rahab the Harlot?

C. Limley Gilbert? Or ...

D. Jesus Christ?

If you answered, "D. Jesus Christ", you answered correctly. Yep, sweet and cuddly, seven-pound, thirteen-ounce, baby Jesus lambasted these strutting religious nabobs with a not very nice *nom de plume* (Mt. 12:34; Mt. 23:33).

John and Jesus cut these jaundiced, hypocritical jackanapes, zero slack. As in, none.

Aside from saying these two clown troops were the sons of Satan, John also said that the wrath of God, which we don't hear much about anymore, is fixin' to flatten them.

Not being a total Jonah-like graceless guy, John gives them a threefold conditional out.

Produce fruit consistent with repentance. In other words, do a 180 from your religious pomp and circumstance. Cease and desist giving God lip service.

He pummeled them away from claiming religious privilege because of who they were linked to familially.

He said bear biblical fruit or get ready to bear the

# John The Baptist

flames of an eternal hell.

Now you know why most Pharisees and Sadducees didn't frequent John the Baptist's podcast page. John was a holy acid bath, a veritable brutal truth bomb to bad religious actors who love to play pretend with that which is most holy.

# Chapter Seven: John Goes Medieval on an Evil Politician

*And King Herod heard about it, for His (Jesus) name had become well known; and people were saying, "John the Baptist has risen from the dead, and that is why these miraculous powers are at work in Him." But others were saying, "He is Elijah." And others were saying, "He is a prophet, like one of the prophets of old." But when Herod heard about it, he kept saying, "John, whom I beheaded, has risen!"*

*For Herod himself had sent men and had John arrested and bound in prison on account of Herodias, the wife of his brother Philip, because he had married her. For John had been saying to Herod, "It is not lawful for you to have your brother's wife." And Herodias held a grudge against him and wanted to put him to death, and could not do so; for Herod was afraid of John, knowing that he was a righteous and holy man, and he had been protecting him. And when he heard him, he was very perplexed; and yet he used to enjoy listening to him. An opportune day came when Herod, on his birthday, held a banquet for his nobles and military commanders, and the leading people of Galilee; and when the daughter of Herodias herself came in and danced, she pleased Herod and his dinner guests; and the king said to the girl, "Ask me for whatever you want, and I will give it to you." And he swore to her, "Whatever you ask of me, I will give it to you, up to half of my kingdom." And she went out and said to her mother, "What shall I ask for?" And she said, "The head of John the Baptist." Immediately she came in a hurry to the king and asked, saying, "I want you to give me at once the head of John the Baptist on a platter." And although the king was very sorry, because of his oaths and his dinner guests, he was unwilling to refuse her. Immediately the king sent an executioner and commanded him to bring back his head. And he went and beheaded him in the prison, and brought his head on a platter, and gave it to the girl; and the girl gave it to her mother. When his disciples heard about this, they came and carried away his body, and laid it in a tomb.*

*– Mark 6: 14-29 (NASB)*

# John The Baptist

I used to be a part of a cadre of ministers who thought the pinnacle of success was to hang around political leaders. They loved to have their pics taken with them, or have them write blurbs for their milk-and-water books, or be invited by them to say the opening prayer to their ghastly satanic soiree. OMG, folks. They'd swoon over politicos. I mean, swoon. They'd never stop talking about meeting them afterward, either.

I was discussing that milk-livered mess with a person the other day, and they responded that the late great Billy Graham, also hung out with many, many heads of state. I acknowledged that Mr. Graham sure did but he also preached the gospel to them and called them to repentance. There's a big difference between photo-ops for personal glory with putrid politicians and an opportunity seized upon, like Graham did, to try to get a leader to repent and to turn to God.

One thing's for certain: When John was tooling around this blue marble, he kissed zero political backside. He wasn't starstruck by some dude's kingship. John couldn't turn the "prophet" off in himself. If he smelt methane gas emanating from someone's soul he was going to pull out his turn-or-burn sledgehammer and let fly on whoever needed a righteous walloping.

Ergo, my beloved, John the Baptist didn't turn a blind eye to King Herod's adultery with his brother's wife Herodias. He rebuked him for it. Most ministers today would've let it slide. Here would be their reasoning ...

1. "Well, you see, I shouldn't rebuke him now, but I shall wait 'til I have a better relationship with King Herod so I will have earned his trust in order to speak into his life. As Steve Covey said, I would 'seek first to understand Herod and not to be understood by Herod.'"

2. Or maybe, they wouldn't rebuke King Herod because his current wife is a real Joy Behar and Herodias meets his soul and sexual needs better than Broomhilda ever did, and anyways, who are we to judge?

3. Or, here's a path often taken by the hip, PC-pastors of The Church of The Poisoned Mind: "I will not confront Herod about his sin of adultery, but I will exhort him instead to find his purpose in life, to be a man of destiny and to live his best life now. That's more positive than telling this powerful leader that he's an adulterer that needs to repent. That old-school gospel stuff John and Jesus preached is so rude, eh?"

As you read at the top of this chapter, John the Baptist called King Herod out on his crap just like Elijah jet-blasted Ahab and his wife Nancy Pelosi. I mean ... Jezebel.

Elijah, of whom Jesus likened John in regards to his epic wrecking crane ministry gift (Mt. 11:7-14), was also no fan of foul politicians. Matter of fact, Elijah's calling was to confront corrupt leaders. His work was not to start orphanages. He didn't feed the poor. He didn't have a leprosy outreach. He didn't start an effort to save abused camels. He was not a life coach with a Christian flare. He was not a fashionable and swanky prophet. He didn't seek to be a positive, motivational speaker trying to subtly blend God's message into the corrupt culture by getting a haircut like Ahab, dressing like the backslidden Israelites, and going to formal state dinners.

Screw that noise. That was not Elijah. His job: scalp corrupt leaders who were leading his country astray.

Indeed, Elijah's call was not to sing kum-ba-yah. His work was to pronounce judgment on Jezebel and her jacked-up ilk. If Elijah had done anything else, like dog rescues, or marital counseling, or hospital visitations, he would have been in direct disobedience to the call of God. No, Elijah was a biblical badass because he stayed focused and did something that all the other prophets were scared to do, namely confront wicked rulers. Would to God that we had some Elijahs and John the Baptists doing that today both to the Left and the Right.

Elijah was different because he had an attitude, and this attitude was a threat to all that was evil. He was a hazard to cultural constructs that would keep him and those God loved dumb and down and beholden to shady leaders. Elijah was not a dutiful and domesticated ecclesiastical cow of the politically and culturally correct constructs.

And our beloved, John the Baptist, sported that same prophetic throat-puncher gift when it came to putrid politicians.

As you can imagine, that type of ministry, rebuking powerful wicked leaders, comes with a cost. The cost to John was jail time and decapitation – of which Jesus did nothing to spare John from either.

In summation, little children, I shall close this chapter with a quote from Joseph Parker.

> *The man whose little sermon is "repent"*
> *sets himself against his age, and will for the*
> *time being be battered mercilessly by the age*
> *whose moral tone he challenges. There is but*
> *one end for such a man – "off with his head!"*
> *You had better not try to preach repentance*
> *until you have pledged your head to heaven.*

*(\*Well, I thought I was finished with this chapter but I just had to add this chunk of meat regarding pastors and politicians from my bestselling book, "The Wildman Devotional: A 50 Day Devotional for Men." Enjoy.)*

The Apostle Paul says, with zero ambiguity …

*Don't become partners with those who reject*
*God. How can you make a partnership out*
*of right and wrong? That's not partnership;*
*that's war. Is light best friends with dark?*
*Does Christ go strolling with the Devil?*

— 2 Cor. 6:14-15 (TM)

# John The Baptist

I've heard Pastors say, "It doesn't matter who a Christian votes for or what political party they support. We're just called to love Jesus." Uh, sorry Pastor Disaster. That's spiritual-sounding *skubalon.*

I think it does matter. If a politician or political party is cool with ...

1. Murdering unborn babies (Hos. 13:16; Ez. 23:29).

2. Same-sex marriage (Rom. 1:18-28; Mt. 19:3-6).

3. Teaching five- to nine-year-olds that sodomy and transgenderism are great (Lk. 17:1-2).

4. Declaring only white people are pure evil when everyone, outside of Christ, is radically corrupt (Rom. 3:9-18).

5. Bowing to godless foreign countries that hate America (Ez. 28:9).

6. Allowing a lawless invasion of our Southern border (1Tim. 1:9).

7. Being unable to define what a woman is (Gen. 1:26-28).

8. Big dudes competing against smaller women in sports (Prov. 20:23).

9. Forcing little children to wear ineffective face masks and take ineffective vaccines (2Jn. 12).

10. Publicly booing God at their National Convention (Isa. 1:4; Prov 24:24).

If a political party does the aforementioned, (and supports many other anti-biblical policies) then they are officially raging against righteousness and a Christian would be sinning if they supported that garbage (Prov. 4:14; Jas. 4:17)

Governments are supposed to protect and praise what is good and punish what is evil. That's "good and evil" as defined by the word of God and not Netflix (Rom. 13:1-5; 1Pet. 2:13-15). When a government ceases to do that then the Christian is duty-bound not to support those less than civil magistrates (Acts 5:29). Indeed, like John the Baptist, they should rebuke them and expose them for their blatant evil deeds.

Finally, I'll end this epic chapter with a few softball questions. What would John the Baptist say to a pastor who praised a politician who was for …

1. Abortion on demand, up to full term, at the taxpayers expense?

2. Joe Biden's disastrous, "Build Back Better Act"?

3. Loosey-goosey voting regulations?

4. Dudes competing in girls' sports?

5. Open borders. Which means increased crime, chaos, and drug cartels?

6. Expanding the power of the government and the expense of our personal liberties?

7. Disallowing parents to choose where their kids go to school?

8. Drag Queens twerking and proselytizing little kids at the public library with their twisted take on life?

So, what do you imagine John the Baptist would say to a pastor who supported that anti-Christian tawdry tripe? Would John comment at all? Would John let it slide? Or, would John let fly some holy invective at said minister? I'm going with the latter. One thing I do know for certain is that John wouldn't praise the "pastor" and/or the politician who supported such demonic garbage.

# Chapter Eight. The University of Earth, Wind & Fire

*Now in those days John the Baptist came,
preaching in the wilderness of Judea, saying, "Repent, for the kingdom of heaven is
at hand." For this is the one referred to by
Isaiah the prophet when he said, "The voice
of one calling out in the wilderness, 'Prepare
the way of the Lord, Make His paths straight!'*

– Matthew 3:1-3 (NASB)

As you well know by now, I think it's hilarious
whom God chose to introduce His Son to the
planet, i.e. an unorthodox holy wildman. I also think
it's funny where God chose to stage this event, namely … in the wilderness of Judea.

Every Christian know-it-all, every whizbang Christian marketing guru, and all savvy social media influencers would not have chosen John and they wouldn't have chosen a desert and a muddy creek to formally launch Jesus's earthly ministry. You and I both know that's true.

But God did.

Good stuff coming out of a wild place is definitely a consistent, funky bottom-line bass note that's played both in the Old Testament and the New.

When God goes shopping for prophets, liberators and lawgivers, righteous kings and judges, one can regularly find Him looking for love in all the wrong religious places, namely … the wilderness.

For example, when God needed a liberator and a lawgiver to defy Pharaoh and emancipate a massive slave labor workforce, He went to the wilderness and found an unconfident octogenarian, who had a sucky job, and was on the lam from a murder he had committed four decades ago. His name was Moses.

In addition, when God needed someone to eternally shut the mouth and sever the head off of a smack-talking monstrous Philistine, He again found a teenage assassin working in the sandbox of the wilderness. His name was David.

Do you need another example? You do? Okay. Here's one: Elijah. Elijah was a Tishbite. He was from Tishbe. Have you ever heard of Tishbe? Yeah, me neither. Tishbe was a mountainous region in Gilead. Gilead lay on the fringes of Israel ergo, it really doesn't figure in too much in biblical history. Zero is known about Tishbe. Nada is known about Elijah prior to his *tete-a-tete* with Jezebel. Elijah just shows up, from the wilderness, talking mad smack to the King and Queen about a punitive drought that's about to slap the land for three years because Ahab's a wuss who married a Baal-worshiping pagan chick who would've meshed well with the coven of *The View.*

So, why does God go hunting for leaders in the wilderness? Here's my two cents ...

**Number One:** Aside from the natural noises from chirping crickets, singing songbirds, screeching eagles, clashing rams, roaring lions, bubbling brooks, and mooing cattle, the wilderness, by and large, is pretty quiet.

If you're going to hear, "Thus says the Lord", you're going to need some peace and quiet. Y'know what we don't have much of anymore in our post-modern paranormal state of noise, noise, noise? That would be big blocks of *silencio.* Most people go nuts if they don't have something noisy going on around them. I saw a new app on my TV that allows the viewer to watch four different football games at once as if we didn't already have the attention span of a ferret on a double espresso.

While penning this part of the book about the need for silence for the making of a prophet my phone starts blowing up with alerts. Email alert. Text message alert. DM alert. Instagram alert. Signal alert. Etherium alert. Truth Social alert. Twitter alert. Guess what I did? I went to my iPhone's home screen, swiped down and then hit airplane mode. If you and I are going to get in tune with what God is saying and doing, we're gonna have to get away, get alone, and get quiet with God and His Word. That's one reason I believe God went shopping in the desert for His dudes: they were unplugged from all the noise and tuned into Him.

**Number Two:** Another thing the wilderness represents is brokenness. The wilderness has ways of humbling us haughty critters to show us how puny we are without all of our little gadgets and props.

The wilderness Moses walked through and worked in morphed him from being a self-assertive Egyptian stud to a broken old man with zero foreseeable opportunities. It took this great undoing of Moses to make Moses, Moses. Oh, and by the way, this undoing of Moses was not short-lived. As T. Austin Sparks said,

"Moses must go into the wilderness and for forty years be emptied out, until there is nothing left of all that as a basis upon which he can have confidence to do the work of God or fulfill any Divine commission. He was by nature a man, "mighty in words and works"; and yet now he says, 'I am not eloquent … I am slow of speech...'" (Ex. 4:10)

The wilderness brought Moses down to his zero point which made him perfect for God to use now. Now it's all of God and none of Old Mo.

**Number Three:** The wilderness brings a much-needed rawness to the prophet and the Message. There's something about the wilderness that melts the plastic blather from our spirit. One hundred and fifty years ago, one had to learn the ways of the wild or they'd die. The wilderness is uncultivated. It's not manicured by some coy florist. It's untailored. It's raw. It's real. It's beautiful and it's deadly. It declares God's glory in spectacular ways (Ps. 19; Rom. 1). It's not safe. It can be comfortable and it can make you wanna run home to yo' mama. King David said God restored his beat-up soul, not in a conference, not via Instagram, not in a support group, or on a Zoom chat, but by lying down in green pastures by still waters (Ps. 23). That would be outdoors, folks. I think it is definitely worth noting, dear indoor Christian, that a stack of God's epic hell-razers, were deeply connected to God via the rawness of nature. King David and his son Solomon, when they wrote divinely inspired Psalms and Proverbs, they drew heavily off the natural order for eternal wisdom. There's a big difference between a man who has been impacted by hurricanes, tornadoes, volcanic eruptions, floods, earthquakes, giant dust storms, nature's beauty, the wilderness' starkness and its raw power, and the dude who dwells inside, under fluorescent lights, watching TikTok videos, whose only form of exercise is jogging his memory or masturbating. Wouldn't it be great if the next move of God came through hunters and hunting guides, anglers and fishing captains, mountain climbers and farmers and ranchers who've spent the last twenty to forty years hanging out with God out in the woods and/or on the open seas? I think it would. There's definite precedence for that leadership selection. God loved utilizing His outdoor boys. His Son, Jesus, spent a bunch of time getting regular doses of the irregular wild, in between casting out demons, healing the sick, and preaching the Good News. Maybe, we should be like Jesus and get outdoors more. It'll keep your message real, raw, and oh-so-relevant.

**Number Four:** I'm not a betting man, but I'm a guessin' that the wilderness was a lonely place. As stated, some of the time spent in the wild by several of God's chosen men spanned anywhere from a decade to forty frickin' years. Yikes, eh? Yep, these dudes, like John the Baptist, were not social butterflies. They were big-time into social distancing. God was undoing them, and making them over an extended period of time. And to get what He wanted out of them, ministry-wise, He had to have these men fly solo for many, many moons. That was their schooling. Just them, the creative element, and the Creator, of course. I know people who freak out if they're not doing something with someone 24/7/365 either in person or online. They're not comfortable being alone with God. I'm sorry, dear Christian, but if you want God to use you greatly, it's going to require big chunks of time with just you and Him. Leonard Ravenhill once told me when I was a young Christian that it will take twenty years for me to become a man of God. I hated that notion. I wanted to be one immediately. There are no shortcuts with God in the school of the wilderness. By the way, Ravenhill was wrong. It took me thirty years. :P

# John The Baptist

John the Baptist's seminary was one of solitude. One that'll break the nonsense from your soul, through a raw and awe interfacing with the created order, during a long stint of loneliness with just him and the Father. It was a perfect plan because when John graduated from The University of Earth, Wind, and Fire, he shook all of hell.

# Chapter Nine:
# He Has a Demon

*To what then shall I compare the people of this generation, and what are they like? They are like children who sit in the marketplace and call to one another, and say, 'We played the flute for you, and you did not dance; we sang a song of mourning, and you did not weep.' For John the Baptist has come neither eating bread nor drinking wine, and you say, 'He has a demon!' The Son of Man has come eating and drinking, and you say, 'Behold, a gluttonous man and a heavy drinker, a friend of tax collectors and sinners!' And yet wisdom is vindicated by all her children.*

*– Luke 7:31-35 (NASB)*

Here's a great quote for a refrigerator magnet: "Legalists look for reasons to discount God's messengers."

The cabal Christ is addressing in the aforementioned text were the scriptures' Ultimate Bad Guys, the Pharisees. These haughty murmurers rejected John and Jesus and ultimately slaughtered them both, all in the name of their self-righteous religious rules and regulations (Acts 13:27).

Check it out: When Jesus feasted, drank alcohol, and hung out with naughty boys and girls, they accused Him of gluttony, being a boozer, and running with the devil.

You'd think with that ill-founded critique of Christ, the Pharisees would be all about John's person and work because of his strict asceticism, but you'd be wrong. John's eating and drinking habits are the exact opposite of Jesus' and yet, they said John was demon possessed.

There was no pleasing this scrupulous sect unless you were in lockstep with their Cult of the Absurd. You could not deviate one angstrom from their erroneous path or they would cancel your backside.

John the Baptist couldn't please them.

Jesus couldn't please them.

The Apostles couldn't please them.

# John The Baptist

That means, if you truly follow Christ, the implacable religious do-gooders are going to discount, hate, and talk mad smack about you as well.

So, buckle up buttercup. It's going to get rough.

Jesus' family thought He was nuts. By the way ... that includes the Virgin Mary. Google Mark 3:20,21 and Mark 3:31-34 if you don't believe me.

Jesus' hometown homies neutralized Him because of their familiarity with Him prior to His baptism. Their familiarity, which bred contempt for Christ, effectively cut off the power of God to their town of Nazareth (Mt. 13:53-58). Wow. Talk about a stupid, stupid move.

The addlepated in Corinth, who Paul led to Christ and started their church, turned on Paul and labeled him a phony to such an extent that Paul was forced to defend His apostleship (Read 2 Corinthians 11).

The bottom line is, my beloved reader, spiritually arrogant peeps look for junk on you in order to depreciate you. You cannot please them. Therefore, you shouldn't even bother. They labeled God's preordained forerunner for His Son's ministry a demoniac. I wonder what they'll label you? Who knows? One thing for certain, it won't be flattering.

Self-righteous religious people are some of the meanest bastards on this planet. I used the word *bastards* on purpose because that's what King Jimmy calls them in Hebrews 12:8. Plus, the pearl-clutchers will think that I'm cussing, which will set their heads spinning, even though that word is used three times in sacred scripture according to the King James Version.

Lastly, here's three ways to keep you from falling into the same satanic pit the Pharisees fell into.

When you hear biblical preaching that roasts your flesh …

1. Do you look for reasons to reject its application to you because it rebukes you?

2. Do you pick apart the messenger, or his wife and/or family because that truth bomb he launched landed too close to home?

3. Are you open to instruction and/or correction from someone if they're not your *style* or your particular religious *flavor?*

Fault-finding, grumbling and complaining, division and divisiveness are the traits of the self-righteous and their dad, the Devil. It's the stuff that the Accuser of the Brethren does. It is prideful and "pious" filth. It leads to demonic bondage, cloaked in religious garb. If not repented of, it'll lead a person, or a group, to fight against God's messengers and ultimately send them to hell.

Remember, if John the Baptist was denigrated for not towing their nit-picking do-gooder line, they're going to say the same, or worse, about you. Don't let

# John The Baptist

their words derail you or grind you down. Never forget that critics are like eunuchs in a harem. They're
there every night. They see it done every night. They
know how it should be done every night, but they
can't do it themselves.

# Chapter Ten: Not a Reed Shaken by the Wind

*As these disciples of John were going away, Jesus began speaking to the crowds about John: "What did you go out into the wilderness to see? A reed shaken by the wind?*

– Matthew 11:7 (NASB)

It's funny (not so funny) how pastors cloak their cowardice when it comes to defying ecclesiastical, cultural, and political giants.

When COVID hit, some ministers followed Fauci's orders and shut their churches down. They called their obedience to that homunculus liar, who should be in prison, "gathering wisely." I called what they did, "a God offending, mass delusional psychosis," and I exhorted them to repent or quit pastoring because they failed Christ and their church miserably.

Can you imagine Little Lord Fauci telling John the Baptist ...

1. He's gotta mask up.

2. He must force that mob in the wilderness to social distance.

3. John must take some strange medicine that King Herod's alchemists hurriedly concocted or else Johnny won't get to preach anymore?

JB would've told whatever Prefect who ordered him to do thus-and-such to go suck an egg.

That's what prophets do: they don't budge when threatened inside or outside of the church when they're standing on the Solid Rock of Christ and His Word.

But limp noodle pastors will.

Yep, when culture, politics, or public opinion rages against biblical truth, a lot of pastors curl up in the fetal position and wet their big Christian diaper. After they wet themselves in fear of being disliked, they rose from that ignoble position and quickly morphed into a step-n-fetch for the anti-theists so they won't lose their 501(c)3 or something like that.

John the Baptist was not some frail little daisy

blown by the wind.

John was no spiritual weathervane that would turn whatever direction the popular sentiments blew.

John the Baptist was a prophet and prophets don't curtsy to culture because they're too beholden to God and they fear Him and Him alone (Lk. 12:1-4).

Would that description of John befit you, Dear Pastor?

Or, are you a reed shaken by the wind?

Are you a weak and wavering wittle evangelical weathervane?

Do we need to buy you some silk pajamas?

Being a Christian coward before the thuggish thought police isn't a big deal anymore. Cowardice is not a sin according to The 21st Century Accommodation Church of Capitulation. For instance …

The winds of wokism…

The winds of Marxism…

The winds of rogue politicians…

The winds of fake news…

The winds of bad science…

The winds of false doctrine…

The winds of intimidation…

The winds of domination…

And the winds of manipulation…

Are all blowing at full tilt today and usually, under their gale force, you'll find spineless ministers aplenty just flapping in their breeze instead of defying the evil winds of doctrine and control (Jude 1:12; Eph. 4:14).

It's funny when such ministers do get busted for dancing with one or more of these devils they always have an excuse for why they're bowing to the enemy and why they're ashamed of God's Word.

Although cowardice, or being a reed shaken by the wind, might not be a big whoop any longer in The Church of the New Groove it's still a big vice according to Sacred Scripture.

Matter of fact, Jesus puts the sin of being a coward right up there with: murder, sexual deviancy, black magic, idol worshiping, and all manner of lies, hype, and spin. Do you want me to prove it? Okay, here you go …

> But as for the cowards and the ignoble and the contemptible and the cravenly lacking in courage and the cowardly submissive, and as for the unbelieving and faithless, and as for the depraved and defiled with abominations, and as for murderers and the lewd and adulterous and the practicers of magic arts and the idolaters (those who give supreme devotion to anyone or anything other than God) and all liars (those who knowingly convey untruth by word or deed)—[all of these shall

*have] their part in the lake that blazes with fire and brimstone. This is the second death.*

*– Rev. 21:8 (AMPC)*

Yikes, eh? Again, most little Christians wouldn't have put cowardice in that bedeviled list of the traits of the be-damned, but Jesus did.

The Amplified Bible's expansive definition of the Greek word for cowardice makes it a very, very nasty sin, doesn't it? They render the coward as ...

1. Ignoble: Someone who's base, or below par, or in our vernacular ... They suck.

2. Contemptible: A person who's despicable and worthy of scorn.

3. Cravenly: Someone who is spineless, soft, unheroic, and unmanly.

4. Submissive. A person who yields and gives up their will and their rights. One who is obedient, giving their power and control to another person or party. Essentially, it is someone who'll hand over their brains and balls when asked to by anyone, anywhere, and at any time.

That's how the Triune Godhead sees cowardice

and being ashamed of God's word before godless masses. It. Is. A. MAJOR. Sin.

If you've been afraid to speak the truth, I'd ask God to:

A. Forgive you for being a wuss and …

B. Give you great boldness to not bend in front of the blowhards who expect you to genuflect to their bad ideas.

That's what I do when I've been guilty of being a fear-laden hamster.

To those who excuse and won't confess your cowardice for whatever prideful reason, all I have to say to you is … good luck at the Judgment Seat because you're going to account to a Holy Christ who said the following …

*For whoever is ashamed of Me and My words in this adulterous and sinful generation, the Son of Man will also be ashamed of him when He comes in the glory of His Father with the holy angels.*

– Mk. 8:38 (NASB)

Lord, raise up an army of ministers and believers who, like John the Baptist, are not reeds shaken by the wind.

Can I get an, "Amen"?

# Chapter Eleven: Great in the Eyes of God

*Jesus said, "Truly I say to you, among those born of women there has not arisen anyone greater than John the Baptist!"*

– Matthew 11:11 (NASB)

What's "great" nowadays? Well, let's see. In the United States of Liberal Acrimony this is "great" and celebrated by the Lunatic Left.

1. If you're a six-foot, four-inch, two-hundred-and-fifty pound, twenty-one-year-old dude, who now calls himself Sabrina and currently dominates in women's sports, well then … you're awesome!

2. Those who champion murdering unborn ba-

bies are "great heroes" to the Left's Death Cult.

3. If you're a child-sniffing, half-dead, sleepy, creepy, octogenarian carrier pigeon for radical Marxist ideals you're considered a "great president" by the wombats who worship Soros, China, and Satan, of course.

4. In addition, if you are a drag queen that bumps and grinds in front of terrified eight-year-old school kids, the lascivious Left will sing your praises, give you glory, and deem you a "great they/them."

In Hollywood, you're great if you do the ensuing ...

1. Endorse movies that paint Caucasians as blue-eyed white devils and declare that other races are pure as the driven snow and are owed reparations by the evil crackers. If that's you, then say, "Hello!" to greatness.

2. If you celebrate man-boy love, approve of soft-core porn in Disney movies, and parlay more sex on the silver screen than Sodom & Gomorrah did in the days of yore, then La-la-land deems you fabulous. Indeed, if that's you or your company, then you, my friend, are a *zeitgeist*. Yea, a veritable *au courant* trendsetter for the glorious glitterati.

3. This one will really rack up great points for

you in Tinseltown: If you paint Jesus in some kind of sin-sullied slanderous way then they will love you with mad love. I'm talking about Oscar award-winning approval.

The Church, like the culture, has the same jacked-up definitions of true greatness. In the Church, you're "great" in the eyes of the enfeebled evangelical hosts if you do the following ...

1. If your pastor sports skinny jeans and your church has big screens and smoke machines then ... boom ... you're hot, baby! I said, hot!

2. If you have at least 5,000 people in attendance on Sundays then congratulations ... you're "great".

3. If everyone likes your pastor, then you're "great" in the eyes of today's church especially if you can also make it on to MSNBC.

Even Jesus's disciples, after three years of hearing Him teach, and being personally mentored by God in the flesh, were still carnal to the core when it came to understanding what God deemed truly great. Check it out ...

*And a dispute also developed among them as to which one of them was regarded as being the greatest. And He said to them, "The kings of the Gentiles domineer over them; and those who have authority over them are*

*called 'Benefactors.' But it is not this way
for you; rather, the one who is the greatest
among you must become like the youngest,
and the leader like the servant. For who is
greater, the one who reclines at the table or
the one who serves? Is it not the one who
reclines at the table? But I am among you as
the one who serves.*

*– Lk. 22:24-27 (NASB)*

Jesus told His dunderheaded disciples, who were gunning for greatness, hungry for titles and accolades, that the greatest in the group is the dude who operates as the least privileged junior amongst them. The person whose joyful job it is to serve others more than himself.

Question: How many Christians do you see queued up to take that role of a servant on? Not too many, eh? But Jesus did and via His servant spirit, He was highly exalted. Or as Paul put it …

*Do nothing from selfishness or empty con-
ceit, but with humility consider one another
as more important than yourselves; do not
merely look out for your own personal interests, but also for the interests of others. Have
this attitude in yourselves which was also in
Christ Jesus, who, as He already existed in
the form of God, did not consider equality
with God something to be grasped, but emptied Himself by taking the form of a bond-ser-
vant and being born in the likeness of men.
And being found in appearance as a man, He
humbled Himself by becoming obedient to
the point of death: death on a cross. For this*

*reason also God highly exalted Him, and bestowed on Him the name which is above every name, so that at the name of Jesus every knee will bow, of those who are in heaven and on earth and under the earth, and that every tongue will confess that Jesus Christ is Lord, to the glory of God the Father.*

– Phil. 2:3-11 (NASB)

Let's recount Christ's attitude while He was ministering here amongst us mortals two millennia ago and see how He differs from the vibe in most churches today.

**Number One:** *"... With humility consider one another as more important than yourselves?"*

I hate to seem negative but, you're more likely to see a Yangtze Finless Porpoise swimming in the L.A. River than see evangelicals consider someone else more important than themselves. That's particularly true amongst ministers and Christian "entertainers".

**Number Two:** *"Do not merely look out for your own personal interests, but also for the interests of others."*

Again, that sentiment is very rare within our egoistic ecclesiastical environs.

**Number Three:** *"Empty oneself?"*

Yeah, right. Emptying oneself is selling in evangelical circles about as well as fried horny toad legs slathered with cricket squishin's would on Gwyneth Paltrow's *GOOP* platform.

**Number Four:** *"Take on the form of a servant?"*

Uh … no *gracias,* saith the self-infatuated saint.

**Number Five:** *"Humble oneself to the point of death on a cross?"*

"H … E … double hockey sticks … to the No", cries the fair-weather, supposed follower, of the lowly Nazarene.

However, the aforementioned is what Jesus exemplified, namely: the setting aside of privileges, taking on the status of a slave, and not claiming special rights. Instead, He lived a selfless, obedient life and then died a selfless, obedient death – and the worst kind of death at that – a crucifixion (Phil. 2 TM).

That is true greatness, ladies and gents.

That is what gave Him the highest honor.

God help us all because very, very few people are seeking to attend that School of Christ and yet, that is The Way of our Master.

So, what did John the Baptist embody that made him great in God's eyes? Well, it's stuff like …

i.   John wasn't a puppet of public opinion. He went against the grain, following God, and declaring only what God prompted him to preach. Yep, John had zero reticence in rebuking whomever, wherever, and whenever if they had it coming. He served the Lord in that manner with his prophetic gift.

2. John was cool with being unique and living bold, wild, and free before the Father versus following religious traditions, dietary customs, and stodgy wardrobe trends. You gotta know that God had a great chuckle seeing the stark life contrast between John, God's special boy, and the finical, overly plumed, Pharisees.

3. John's unabashed and brutal honesty when preaching definitely distinguished him from the herd of religious wafflers and warblers of the Temple's bogus and bondage-inducing blather.

4. The fact that John sought to decrease his stature at the apex of his ministry is some weird, wild stuff you don't hear much about amongst the Instagram mavens.

5. John's comfortability with being alone with God for three decades in the desert before a short stint of ministry had to also refresh the Father because that trail is seldom taken by those that claim they know God best.

6. Jesus called this prophet great and yet, he didn't speak in tongues. He performed no miracles. He cast out no demons. He didn't have a Youth Group or an epic Children's Ministry. He's got no money, no prophetic blog, no action pics of him preaching. No massive ministerial RV. No multi-purpose

sanctuary. No YouTube channel. Rome, the Pharisees, and the Sadducees all hated him. He didn't have a 10,000-square-foot mansion and a ministry yacht. He wrote no books and took no selfies and yet, the Son of God said of him ...

*Truly I say to you, among those born of women there has not arisen anyone greater than John the Baptist! Yet the one who is least in the kingdom of heaven is greater than he.*

– Mt. 11:11 (NASB)

At this writing, I just turned sixty years old. At sixty, I care less about the all "ministerial" drivel I did in my thirties. I'm sure there still lurks within my whirring tin brain pockets of inglorious self-love, but at this juncture, I'm concerned less and less about what people think of me and more and more about what God does. I know ... I know ... I'm a slow learner. But at least I'm learning, eh? From an eternal perspective, I'd rather have God's approval than man's. Can you imagine being regarded by religious peeps as being "great and marvelous" and God doesn't think that highly of you? Or worse yet: He declares He doesn't even know you (Mt. 7:23)? That would suck. The only way for you and I to curtail that fate is to, like John the Baptist, live solely before the Audience of One and not for the fickle masses.

# John The Baptist

# Chapter Twelve: You Might Be a Prophet If ...

In 1993 Jeff Foxworthy launched his insanely successful comedy series, "You Might Be A Redneck If ..." which highlighted the whacked things rednecks are known to do. He featured stuff like ...

You might be a redneck if.

- Your mother has ever been involved in a fistfight at a high school sports event.

- Your wife's hairdo has ever been ruined by a ceiling fan.

- Hail hits your house and you have to take it to the body shop for an estimate.

- You know how many bales of hay your car

can hold.

- You view the upcoming family reunion as a chance to meet women.

- You own a homemade fur coat.

- You have a rag for a gas cap.

- You've ever used lard in bed.

- You've ever financed a tattoo.

- You prefer car keys to Q-tips.

- You have an Elvis Jell-O mold.

Yep, if you're guilty of the above, you might be a redneck. Oh, by the way, I know of no rednecks who ever got ticked off at Foxworthy for these hilarious observations. Indeed, rednecks didn't try to have Jeff canceled. On the contrary, they flocked to his shows, bought his CDs, and cherished his joke books. Do you know why they did the aforesaid? Well, it's because they're not snowflakes and they can take a joke. That's why.

Below are twenty-five tale-tell signs that you might be a prophet or have prophetic bents/gifts for the body of Christ. Enjoy.

You might be a prophet if …

- You're combative. A prophet insists on battling bunkum and speaking truth to power with zero regard for honorariums or a Dove

# John The Baptist

Award for being Prophet of the Year.

- You tell the hard truth in tough love.

- You weep before you whip.

- You fight the fog of falsity that envelops us all.

- You love candor and hate duplicity.

- You excel at being blunt.

- You have a well-developed *Stercore Tauri* Detector when it comes to unbiblical church stuff.

- You're more like a *Full Metal Jacket* drill sergeant than a Mr. Rogers.

- You're not so much into predicting the future. Your interest lies in getting people to repent in the present to ward off pending doom.

- You have a divine knack for seeing problems and correcting them boldly with Holy Ghost unction.

- You see as God sees and feel what God feels and you carry the burden of the Lord.

- You tell us the ugly truth about ourselves which radically differs from what we imagine we are when we're under the delusions of demons and self-deception.

- You provoke, rebuke, correct, and exhort folks to righteousness. Yep, your words are like burrs in a saddle, irritating and infuriating, especially if someone refuses to repent.

- You're a pain in the butt to the cozy and complacent clique.

- You will tell folks what they don't want to hear when it is really inconvenient for them.

- You throw up at the thought of being determinedly deaf and dumb.

- You epitomize boldness and heroism.

- You're not a Pollyanna regarding the cost of your calling. That's why you never cry like a baby once you get shunned, imprisoned, or executed.

- You have no personal vendettas involved in your rebukes. Indeed, you seek no pound of flesh. It's not about you, but about God.

- You must speak. God's word is like a fire shut up in your bones. You cannot hold it in (Jer. 20:9)

- You cannot turn the prophetic gift off and on. It always stays on unless God says otherwise.

- You're hated while alive and lauded once dead.

# John The Baptist

- You're committed to believing and declaring God's truth and let the chips fall where they may.

- You stick to God's principles and won't budge.

- You refuse to go along with unbiblical garbage just to get along.

- You utterly resist religious traditions and political policies if they're foreign to God, as He is revealed, through the scripture.

Here's an FYI to folks with a prophetic gift: If a person, or a crowd, or a denomination, or non-denomination, or a political party is denying their transgressions, or they're covering them up, and protecting their devils, they probably won't invite you to their soiree because you'll ruin their potluck dinner. Those organizations will trip over backwards to not have their bullocks pointed out by a prophet. Ergo, my beloved prophetic voice, please note: You'll pay retail for the price of your calling. Few folks will want to pay that steep of a tab. Here's a $64,000 question: Will you summon the heroic courage to pay that price? John the Baptist did.

# Chapter Thirteen: The Benefits of a Rude Awakening

I'll never forget our friends inviting this so-called "Important Christian Couple" to a church where I was speaking. They rocked up but as soon as it was over … poof … they were gone. Once we met up with our friends after the service I asked them where the VIP Christian Dynamic Duo went. They said they left and the wife didn't like me because, and I quote, "I wasn't her style of preacher. I was too matter-of-fact." Yep, she didn't like the cut of my jib. What she didn't say was, "He preached heresy" or "He was boring" because those are two things I try to avoid more than Donald Trump does a wet Rosie O'Donnell french kiss.

Dear Preacher Police: If you have a style, or a manner, or a prerequisite, or a cup of tea, or any type of imperative that must be met before you'll receive instruction or rebuke from a minister then I guarantee God is going to purposefully, if you are His kid, insult you in a surly way, to wake your unbiblical backside up.

The Pharisees and the Sadducees and their wannabe lackeys had a "style". They had religious bells and smells. Veritable incense and nonsense aplenty. They had certain ways and means of preaching and teaching. They had rules to what one could and could not do in the Temple, especially on the Sabbath. Good Lawd! They had many many boxes to check. Matter of fact, they worshiped their customs more than they worshiped God. It's true. Google it.

I've been a Christian now at this writing for thirty-nine years. I've seen and heard all kinds of preaching delivered in all kinds of ways. I've heard sonorous, white, Lutheran preachers preach. I've heard screaming and funny black pastors. I've been on the receiving end of fiery Hispanic hell-fire messages. I've been regaled by hilarious and holy raconteurs of various stripes, colors, and denominations from all over America, Western and Southern Europe, and Africa, and guess what dear reader? I don't have a favorite "style" that I prefer. I dig 'em all. *Vive la différence!* The only thing I give a flibbertigibbet about, when it comes to preaching is, was it sound doctrine? That's it, folks. That's all I care about. I do not care whether said minister dotted my punctilious religious "i's" or crossed all of my persnickety stylistic "t's".

# John The Baptist

Here's something they never told you in Youth Group: If you have a style of religion you worship more than you worship God, then God, via the Holy Spirit, God is going to send someone your way with a message you won't like, through a person you won't dig, to upset your vainglorious applecart. Yep, someone will hit you with a truth bomb which you will deem scurrilous and below your tedious sensibilities.

Check it out: God sent the most tidy group of tightly wound religious wonks, the most irreligious and insulting prophet on the planet namely … John the Baptist.

Here's something terrifying to chew on: Heaven and hell hung in the balance for the Pharisees and Sadducees and it was based on their response to wild John and his savage message. Would they choose to overlook his unpolished appearance and embrace his prickly preaching or blow him off because of his style, or lack thereof? Again, think about it: God purposely put this boorish prophet with his curt communique in front of well-heeled and priggish experts to see if they'd repent of their self-righteousness or harden their hearts because John came off like an impolite caveman.

Some folks took offense at John's person and message and were eternally damned. Others did not get offended at John's gruff directives and were privileged with an entrance into God's eternal Kingdom. Yep, John's person and words, to the puffed-up wizards, were a raw and offensive eternal stench of death. To those broken by John's cannonball message to repent, they perceived that earful as a vital fragrance, life-giving and fresh (2Cor. 2:16). So strange, eh? One group's fate was doomed to a hellish abyss and one group was consigned to an abundant, eternal, life and they all heard the same dispatch from the unpolished prophet.

When I was at college, I had two professors who were very John the Baptist-like in their approach to schooling us young fools. One was my PoliSci prof and the other my Life Drawing instructor. The Political Science professor was from Lagos, Nigeria. He fled that craphole for the States ten years prior to his teaching gig. He wanted to live in a country that had a legit Constitution that provided liberty and the pursuit of happiness for her citizens. He took our Constitution, the Bill of Rights, and our Declaration of Independence oh, so, seriously. If you were an American slack-jawed, gum-smacking young moron, who didn't know our Founding Documents and their original intent then you were in deep yogurt around him. My professor would call you out. He'd scream at people for being ignorant of the roots of our Great Experiment in Self-Governance. And I mean, SCREAM. Coeds ran crying from his class. They'd quit in droves. I came to love his uncouth approach when I finally figured out what he was doing. He was thinning the herd. He wanted to raise the next generation of leaders and not babysit hungover, narcissistic, sorority and fraternity dolts.

My Life Drawing teacher was also similarly wired. He'd weed out the graphic design boys and girls from the Fine Arts' grad track. If you didn't have serious raw artistic talent it was his goal and chief joy to get you the heck out of his class. I'll never forget we were in a three-hour life drawing session and at the end of the class the students had to show off their final renderings of the nude model. He told this one wannabe that if what he depicted were to come off his easel and walk around this room everyone would flee in terror. He had several guys and dolls in tears. He would probably be canceled in today's fragile atmosphere of overt wussification. Yes, Dinky: he was rougher than grandma's breath. I believe he shamed two-thirds of our class that year into quitting within the first couple of weeks. It was awesome watching him separate the sheep from the goats. If you didn't have the chops, or if you did have the skills, or were not serious about classical renderings of the human body, then he made it his job to be your worst nightmare. However, if you had rudimentary talents and pursued excellence, then you had his full attention and expertise at your disposal.

In our soft-focus world of over-niceties we don't see my former professors' brusque behavior as beneficial, but rather bellicose and bad. In addition, we can't or won't imagine our seven pound, thirteen ounce, baby Jesus ever being so crude, rude, and socially unacceptable. But both Jesus and John the Baptist were. They had the Gift of Plain Speaking down pat.

Yep, back in the day, if you were a smug holier-than-thou dweeb, or a rich young ruler, or an oily politician, or some strutting Rico Suave, or a vacillating vixen and you collided with John the Baptist or Jesus; it wasn't going to end well for your flesh and they'd probably come off as "rude" to your exceedingly self-important, impenitent sensibilities.

There's no getting around all the rude/"negative" aspects of the scripture, where God directly, or indirectly, through His prophets or through other providential means, jackhammers His kids when they're being jackasses. If you removed all the rude and raw scriptures from the Bible you'd have a three page leafy pamphlet.

So, exactly what is a "Rude Awakening?" Well, I'm glad you asked, you inquiring mind. Simply put, a rude awakening is a sudden realization of the true/bad state of affairs, having previously been under the illusion that everything was hunky-dory.

For instance, the Pharisees thought they were fine, but they were not. They were headed to hell. Their dad was the Devil. They were completely delusional, spiritually deceived, rotted to the core, but externally … They were "very religious and good conservatives." Here's a FYI: did you know a person can be very religious and vote for the GOP and not be right with God? Anyway … I digress. John's soaking the Pharisees down with the firehose of acidic truths was a last ditch effort to get these haughty legalists' souls plucked from the pending pit.

Ditto with the Sadducees.

The general populace, upon hearing JB's rebukes to the uber-religious and his general call to repentance were also stunned into realizing they must repent or be damned. John's message hit home: they were out of sorts with God and they came in droves asking John, "What do we do" (Lk. 7:10)? John's message made them realize they were jacked up. John didn't tell them, "God loves you and has a wonderful plan for your life." John was more like, "Dude, you're in deep doo-doo. Everything you know, and everything that you're doing, is wrong. God's wrath is against that mess and I highly suggest you do a 180, PDQ" (Author's paraphrase).

The Tax Collectors, who were regarded as the scum of the earth in Israel, were also shocked into repentance. They too were so rattled by John's "rude" preaching that they felt a massive urgency to change. They asked John the same question that the GP did, "What do we do" (Lk. 7:12)?

The soldiers present to hear John's preaching were tactless thugs who joyfully enforced Roman rule with whips and swords, also realized that they were eternally doomed and asked John, "What are we to do, as well" (Lk. 7:14)? Again, and pardon my redundancy, the message that ultimately saved them initially terrified them. Yes, fair reader, the message was, *Turn or Burn*. And guess what Christian Marketing Experts: that message worked and it is what the Bible calls, "Preparing the way for the Lord ... making His paths straight". John was being cruel to be kind, as Nick Lowe would say, and that's exactly what The Doctor ordered.

By the way, who says "What do I do" anymore after a sermon? How many peeps do you know who are so stunned by blunt preaching that they earnestly ask after the sermon, "What should I do?" The folks in earshot of John's call to repentance felt something had to be done. Something had to be remedied immediately. Nowadays it's more like, "What's God going to do for me?" In addition, in our culture there is very little massive life change. People who supposedly said, "Yes, to Jesus" manifest zero fruit in keeping with their so-called repentance.

I predict that if the Church in America is going to experience a revival, a reformation, a renaissance (whatever you wanna call it) it'll first experience a Rude Awakening. The reason being is the American Church, like the world, has a massive entitlement mentality, a Laodicean fascination with stuff, a cowardice before evil politicians and their satanic policies, an aversion to godly duty, an addiction to avarice, and a *laissez faire* attitude regarding the Great Commandment and the Great Commission. In addition to that slop, the Church also sports in spades an allergic reaction to any preaching that steps on their well pedicured toes. Which means, my beloved, some Christians toes are going to get walked on. Remember, the "Rude Awakening" brought to you by John always precedes the "Great Awakening" brought to you by Jesus. True revival can be brutal, especially for the fragile snowflakes who are used to being handled with kid gloves.

A year-and-a-half ago, my friend had an altercation with his wife. She broke several of his ribs, cracked his sternum, and gave him a concussion when she yanked him off the couch, while screaming in his face. To this day, his sternum is still in pain because of her blows. The upshot of her injuries to him was she was performing CPR on him after he suffered a massive heart attack and she helped save his life. And that my friends, is pretty much what prophets like John the Baptist do: they hurt you to heal you. Or as Hosea put it seven-hundred years before Jesus' birth …

> *Come on, let's go back to God. He hurt us, but he'll heal us. He hit us hard, but he'll put us right again. In a couple of days we'll feel better. By the third day he'll have made us brand-new, Alive and on our feet, fit to face him. We're ready to study God, eager for God-knowledge. As sure as dawn breaks, so sure is his daily arrival. He comes as rain comes, as spring rain refreshing the ground.*

*– Hos. 6:1-3 (TM)*

Read that again. Like, real slow.

Alright, let's break it down, shall we?

Before being made, "brand new". Before a time of "refreshing" comes to our lives "as spring rain refreshing the ground" Hosea says these things occurred.

1. God's wayward people turned back to Him. "Come on, let's go back to God." Check it out, *por favor*: No revival without returning back to the Lord. Duh.

2. Hosea said God hurt them before He healed

them. "He hurt us, but he'll heal us. He hit us hard, but he'll put us right again." I'll bet you a $1,000 that scripture is not on a refrigerator magnet for sale via Christian websites. Getting "hurt" and "hit hard" by God sounds like a rude awakening to me. What about you?

3. This hurting by God is what caused His beloved to "feel better", "(be) made brand new", "alive and on our feet", "fit to face Him", "ready to study God", "eager for God-knowledge." Ready to be refreshed, in life by Him, like the spring rain.

I've experienced multiple "Rude Awakenings" in my life. Prior to my conversion, me and my girlfriend and our posse were enjoying a Sammy Hagar concert in Lubbock, Texas. I believe the year was 1981. I don't really know. That part of my life is all a blur.

Anyway, Sammy was plowing through his epic song list and we were headbanging along with him while smoking Snoop Dogg-sized amounts of weed, as we plied our livers with a metric-ton of booze. At that juncture, I was nineteen, extremely cocky, with a pretty girlfriend, and a wicked 4-speed Z28. In addition to that, I had a legendary mullet, which I finished off with a red Flashdance headband, and of course my t-shirt was of the sleeveless variety. Yes, my beloved … I was Beavis. Please Note: I was not pondering the afterlife. I was not searching for my destiny, or purpose. I was not on a spiritual quest. I wasn't seeking Jesus. Matter of fact, Christianity was nowhere

# John The Baptist

near my "To Do List." My life was all about sex, drugs, and rock-n-roll, 24/7/365 and I never planned on pumping the brakes on that accident waiting to happen. So, I'm at the concert and Sammy goes into a song from his album, *Street Machine*. The song is titled, *Planet's On Fire*. I had heard that song many times before but that night ... "I heard it" ... "heard it", if you know what I mean. My eyes, ears, soul, and spirit were awakened and sober to its message and it was not good news for me. Here's the lyrics ...

*Planet's On Fire*

*Canceled flights, limousines,*
*Hustle bustles, crazy scenes.*
*First, you're here, then, you're there*
*Pretty soon, man, you've been everywhere.*
*Ooh, this planet's on fire*
*Oh, Satan's desire*
*We've seen the rise, we'll see the fall*
*He's here to see us all,*
*Burn in hell.*
*Time ticks away, faster, faster.*
*You run so fast you forget what you're after.*
*You make a deal to sell your soul*
*Just to find out, baby, it's been sold.*
*Ooh, this planet's on fire*
*Oh, Satan's desire*
*We've seen the rise, we'll see the fall*
*He's here to see us all,*
*Burn in hell.*
*Burn in hell.*

# Doug Giles

*Not me, baby!*
*Ooh, this planet's on fire*
*Oh, Satan's desire*
*We've seen the rise, we'll see the fall*
*He's here to see us all,*
*Burn in hell.*
*Fine, white lines of crystal light*
*Keep us up all day and all night.*
*Oh, we just forgot girls and boys*
*Who thrive on cosmic toys.*
*Ooh, this planet's on fire*
*Oh, Satan's desire*
*We've seen the rise, we'll see the fall*
*He's here to see us all,*
*Burn in hell.*
*Burn in hell, Ow!*
*(This planet's on fire)*
*(This planet's on fire)*
*Ooh, this planet's on fire*
*Oh, Satan's desire*
*Ooh, this planet's on fire*
*Oh, Satan's desire, yeah!*
*Yes!*

To recap: I, Doug Giles, Idiot Emeritus, was a drug-addled moron with zero intentions to desist from that godless glidepath, heard in my spirit something I had never heard before even though I heard and sang that song many times. It was this ...

*"Ooh, this planet's on fire*
*Oh, Satan's desire*
*We've seen the rise, we'll see the fall*

# John The Baptist

*He's here to see us all,*
*Burn in hell."*

Right then and there, the Holy Spirit hit me with conviction. It was not gentle and sweet. It was not a nudge or a suggestion. It was a short and succinct message of … you're going to hell if you don't change. It was clear as crystal and applied to me directly in no uncertain way. Satan was here to see me burn in hell. This was no longer a cool, jammin', abstract song. It was personal and God used a rock-n-roll tune to tune me up to the fact that I was under the wrath of God and things were only going to get eternally worse if I don't repent. It was a rude awakening. I'd like to say that I got saved then and there, but it took another two years of me fighting with God before He conquered me and dragged me into His fold which was a Great Awakening for this rebel without a clue. God's mercy, love, forgiveness, and grace is a GREAT thing to those who are condemned and damned, veritable prisoners of the flesh and devils, who're without hope and estranged from God's covenant.

Since my conversion back in 1983, I've been hit with a few more "rude awakenings" that were not very pleasant at all. Most of them were of my own making. Y'know, God's heavenly chastisement for my earthly stupidity. Other rude awakenings came through satanic attacks via his fleshly followers who love to make Christians' lives miserable. I won't bore you with the details, but I will end with this: No matter how painful, brutal, or rude the crapola is you're currently sloggin' through, you must understand that pain is a pathway to healing according to the word of God. God doesn't mind if a person, church, or nation gets hammered or rebuked because He knows that there's a great awakening on the tail end of that rude awakening for those who "have ears to hear." Ergo, my beloved, embrace the rude, the raw, and the real – even if it bites your flesh and makes you squirm. Our good God has some great things in store for His Church, but to get us where He needs us, sometimes, oftimes, He must shake and bake us before He shapes and remakes us for His glory. Or as the psalmist put it …

*You who have shown me many troubles and distresses, will revive me again, and will bring me up again from the depths of the earth. May You increase my greatness and turn to comfort me.*

– Ps. 71:20-21 (NASB)

# John The Baptist

# Chapter Fourteen: I Called and You Refused

Here's a warning to those rebelling against God's rude awakening in their life. Y'know … those who're blowing off His rebuke and His call to repentance. This is a chunk of scripture I've never heard preached on in your typical Aren't We All Fabulous Church. It is a terrifying passage. Here's Solomon's rude awakening for individuals, churches, cities, states and nations. I would not want to be on the receiving end of this.

*Wisdom shouts in the street,*

*She raises her voice in the public square;*

*At the head of the noisy streets she cries out;*

*At the entrance of the gates in the city she*

*declares her sayings:*

*"How long, you naive ones, will you love simplistic thinking?*

*And how long will scoffers delight themselves in scoffing*

*And fools hate knowledge?*

*Turn to my rebuke,*

*Behold, I will pour out my spirit on you;*

*I will make my words known to you.*

*Because I called and you refused,*

*I stretched out my hand and no one paid attention;*

*And you neglected all my advice*

*And did not want my rebuke;*

*I will also laugh at your disaster;*

*I will mock when your dread comes,*

*When your dread comes like a storm*

*And your disaster comes like a whirlwind,*

*When distress and anguish come upon you.*

*Then they will call on me, but I will not answer;*

*They will seek me diligently but will not find me,*

*Because they hated knowledge*

*And did not choose the fear of the Lord.*

*They did not accept my advice,*

*They disdainfully rejected every rebuke from me.*

*So they shall eat of the fruit of their own way,*

*And be filled with their own schemes.*

*For the faithlessness of the naive will kill them,*

*And the complacency of fools will destroy them.*

– Pr. 1:20-32 (NASB)

That's one of the most horrifying scriptures in the Holy Bible. God tries to wake a people up through reproof, rebuke, and correction; stuff also known as … a rude awakening … and look at their responses:

- They refused to learn from the Lord.

- They turned a deaf ear to God.

- They're ignoring His efforts to wake them the heck up.

- They laugh at His counsel.

- They make jokes about His advice.

- They hated His knowledge.

- They wanted nothing to do with the fear of

God.

So God, effectively says …

- I'll mock you in your troubles and hard times.

- When your life falls apart, you'll need Me then, but don't expect to find Me.

- No matter how hard you look, you won't find Me.

- You wouldn't take My advice and you brushed aside all my offers to train you so, enjoy doing life on your own.

- You've made your bed, now lie in it; you wanted your own way now, so … how do you like it now?

Again, that's the stuff the pastors never tell you at Youth Group and yet, there it is in black and white. Yep, according to Solomon, by inspiration of the Holy Ghost, it does not go well for a person or a people group who ignores God's attempts to wake them up and bring them into His kingdom. This is exactly what happened to the Pharisees and the Sadducees who mocked John the Baptist's attempts to rouse them to repentance. They scoffed at John & God and God scoffed back at them for all eternity (Mt. 23:35-36).

If God's calling you to repentance, I'd repent. I

# John The Baptist

don't care how much it might embarrass you, just do it. God's gracious and ready to forgive and restore the broken-hearted but He has a zero-tolerance policy for self-contented, smug, religious actors who cover up their sin with a religious cloak.

# Addendum:
# Born to Be Wild

John the Baptist was wild. He came from the wilderness and it showed. His clothes were wild. His food selection was wild and his message was wild. Nothing about John was bland, calm, delicate, mellow, moderate, smooth, soft, tepid, blah, dainty, faint, genial, ho-hum, lukewarm, medium, mollifying, pablum, or beige. John the Baptist was pure, uncut, high voltage, Holy Ghost, rock-n-roll.

Yep, John did not fit in the fashionable religious mode. He was uncultivated. He wasn't a product of human aid or human care. He was not subject to restraint or regulation except by God. He was aggressive in nature and impossible to domesticate. He was unpredictable and temperamental. You couldn't saddle John or milk him. You weren't going to be able to put a ring in John's nostrils unless he wanted you to. Oh, and by the way, God purposely hardwired him like that.

Most Christians are the exact opposite of John. They're civilized, cultured, nice, refined, sophisticated, behaved, calm, controllable, delicate, gentle, manageable, orderly, and tame. They're born to be mild, not born to be wild. Matter of fact, here's their favorite song.

*Born to Be Mild*
(To be sung to the tune of, *Born to Be Wild,* by Steppenwolf)

*Get my silky blankie*
*Cry out for my mommy*
*Looking for some comfort*
*In whatever comes my way*

*Yeah, darlin' I won't make it happen*
*I abuse God's love and grace*
*Got rid of my guns at once*
*And fell flat on my face*

*I like pigs in blankets*
*Tightie whitey undies*
*Passing lots of wind.*
*And gooey banana sundaes*

*Yeah, darlin' I won't make it happen*

# John The Baptist

*I abuse God's love and grace*
*Got rid of my guns at once*
*And fell flat on my face*

*Like a true subpar child*
*I was born*
*Born to be mild*
*I can't climb so high*
*I not even gonna try*

*Born to be mild*
*Born to be mild*

Indeed, with most of the brethren in the icky recesses of evangelicalism, you can saddle them and ride them. Very few will ever shock you in any holy form or fashion.

John, however, was shocking to The Behaved's sensibilities.

Jesus was a scandalous offense to The Refined's rationale.

That's why they killed them, folks. They committed the crime of being biblical which, by its very nature, disallowed them to fit into some screwy and satanic religious robotic mode of lackluster domesticity.

They were anything but normal.

You know who else was a wild child? King David was. As a ruddy teenager he killed and decapitated the champion of the Philistines, Goliath (1Sam. 17:48-51). That ain't normal teenage behavior. Aside from that nugget, David also danced in his underwear during a public worship service (2Sam. 6:14). Can you imagine what the pearl-clutchin' evangelicals would say about that? In addition, David cut two hundred foreskins off his enemy's naughty bits as a goof and as a gift for his future father-in-law (1Sam. 18:27). Again, that ain't normal Christian behavior.

Speaking of David.

Out of one hundred and fifty Psalms, or "Palms", as Joe Biden calls them, there are forty "Famous" Psalms according to the experts. Y'know, classics like, "The Lord is my shepherd ..." Psalm 23?

The one we're going to look at in this final chapter didn't make the "famous" cut but I think it deserves a gander because it too is inspired by the Holy Spirit and it fits in *muy bueno* within the topic of this tornadic tome. Y'all ready? Let's roll.

The Psalm is the ninety-second Psalm and the verse I'm gonna put under the microscope is verse ten. Check it out ...

*But You have exalted my horn like that of the wild ox; I have been anointed with fresh oil.*

– Ps. 92:10 (NASB)

Have you ever heard that verse preached on? You have if you attend the Church that I pastor. But I'm a guessin' if you go to your typical Sacchariferous Christian Fellowship you didn't even know it existed.

By the way, why are big chunks of the Bible never touched on nowadays in our sassy, easy-breezy-summer-squeezy, churches? I'll tell you why. *El Diablo* wants you in the dark so you don't morph into a major pain-in-the-butt to him. Anyway, I'm derailing. Back to Psalm 92:10.

In Psalm 92:10 David said, " *... You have exalted my horn like that of the wild ox; I have been anointed with fresh oil."*

The Message Translation renders it thus, *"But you've made me strong as a charging bison ... "*

David said God blessed him to be like a "wild bull" ... "a charging wild bull."

Please note that David didn't say, "The Lord has exalted my horn like that of a Tufted Titmouse: I have been anointed with formaldehyde." When God blessed, favored, and aided His special boy David, He made him roll like a wild ox, like a wild bull, like a wild buffalo. Can you feel that? The "wild bull" blessing is what David deemed an "anointing of fresh oil."

I've been fortunate to have hunted four types of wild bovine here in the U.S. and in Africa. I've hunted the American Bison twice. I've hunted free-range Watusi twice. I have hunted Asiatic Water Buffalo twice. I've hunted Africa's Cape Buffalo three times and I've accompanied my buddy Glenn on four of his Cape Buffalo hunts also in Africa. I can tell you this with great certainty: hunting the wild bulls is anything but dull. Especially Cape Buffalo. The Cape

Buffalo is nobody's fool. They weigh around 1,600-2,000 pounds. They stand about five-and-a-half feet at the shoulder. They're eleven-plus feet long, minus their tail. Yes, Dinky ... they are this thing called big. They're also vicious if wounded or cornered. Their nickname is, "Africa's Black Death." They are a veritable widowmaker. Outdoor writer, the late Robert Ruark, famously said that, "The Cape Buffalo looks at you like you owe him money." So, why are the Cape Buffalo so keyed up and deadly? Well, unlike their American cousins, who have no major apex predators pursuing them, the Cape Buffalo are the favorite table fare for the African lion.

In Africa there's a group of animals called "The Big Five." This company consists of the lion, the leopard, the rhino, the elephant, and the cape buffalo and all five of them are deemed, "Africa's Most Dangerous Game." When you hunt them there's a good chance if you don't do it right you could be pushing up daisies at the end of your safari. Indeed, the wild ox clan have a nasty reputation of making short work of their adversaries. I saw on YouTube the other day some dumb chick in Yellowstone trying to take a selfie with a bison. She thought it was cute how close she was getting to the bull. She was giggling and snapping pics. With each photo she'd inch closer and closer to the buffalo. What she didn't notice, as she was selecting a filter that would decrease how decrepit she looked on Instagram, the bull started pawing the ground. Yep, the bison had enough of her encroachment on his majestic presence and gored her in the crotch and tossed her like a ragdoll into the top of a big ol' cedar tree.

# John The Baptist

So, what's my point? Well, it's this my beloved: God wants to bless you with a dangerous wild bull anointing that'll stomp satanic lions, crush demonic strongholds, and annihilate all threats to that which is holy, just, and good.

For the mild, little safe and dainty Christians that think I'm a bubble-off-level with my musings about God wanting to make you like a wild bull please observe what the Godhead is likened to in this book called *"The Bible."*

*God is not a man, that He would lie,*

*Nor a son of man, that He would change His mind;*

*Has He said, and will He not do it?*

*Or has He spoken, and will He not make it good?*

*20 Behold, I have received a command to bless;*

*When He has blessed, I cannot revoke it.*

*21 He has not looked at misfortune in Jacob;*

*Nor has He seen trouble in Israel;*

*The Lord his God is with him,*

*And the joyful shout of a king is among them.*

*22 God brings them out of Egypt,*

*He is for them like the horns of the wild ox.*

— Num. 23:19-22 (NASB)

Did you catch that last verse ... *"He is for them like the horns of the wild ox."* Balaam compared God to a wild ox with wicked death-dealing horns and tremendous, stomp-a-mud-hole-in-your-chest muscle power. Make that a refrigerator magnet. Check it out. Pharaoh and his doomed armies got the wild ox treatment. They were savagely destroyed in the Red Sea by God in a wild ox fashion. Do you need another example of God being likened to a wild ox? You do? Cool. Here you go ...

> *God brings him out of Egypt,*
>
> *He is for him like the horns of the wild ox.*
>
> *He will devour the nations who are his adversaries,*
>
> *And will crush their bones ...*
>
> – Num. 24:8 (NASB)

Jesus, The Horn of Salvation (Lk. 1:69), was a brutal wild ox to the powers of darkness. If you don't believe me then email Michelle Whitedove and ask her to contact Satan for his comments on what Christ did to him and his ilk.

The Apostles, who are also likened to ox (1Cor. 9:9), were a full-on, wild bull, fierce disaster to Satan's devices.

God's true anointing will make you a wild menace to those with wicked machinations, just like our beloved wildman, John the Baptist.

The Wild Ox anointing will make you ...

• Disobey the Devil.

• Disobey your flesh.

• Disobey bad government.

• Disobey bad religion (Job 39:9-12).

Will you dare to ask God to do for you what He did for David, namely turn you into a holy wild ox for His glory?

> *"But You have exalted my horn like that of the wild ox; I have been anointed with fresh oil."*
>
> – Ps. 92:10 (NASB)

Or will you remain a mild, pusillanimous, domesticated, Christian milk cow?

The choice is yours.

# Doug Giles

## About the Author

Doug earned his Bachelor of Fine Arts degree from Texas Tech University and his certificates in both Theological and Biblical Studies from Knox Theological Seminary (Dr. D. James Kennedy, Chancellor). Giles was fortunate to have Dr. R.C. Sproul as an instructor for many classes.

Doug Giles is the host of *The Doug Giles Podcast*, the co-founder and co-host of the *Warriors & Wildmen Podcast* (1M+ downloads) and the man behind ClashDaily.com. In addition to driving ClashDaily.com (300M+ page views), Giles is the author of several #1 Amazon bestsellers. His book *Psalms of War: Prayers That Literally Kick Ass* (2021) spent 26 weeks at #1 on Amazon. In 2018, Giles was permanently banned from his two-million followers on Facebook.

Doug is also an artist and a filmmaker and his online gallery can be seen at DougGiles.Art. His first film, *Biblical Badasses: A Raw Look at Christianity and Art*, is available via DougGiles. Art.

Doug's writings have appeared in several other print and online news sources, including Townhall.com,The Washington Times,The Daily Caller, Fox Nation, Human Events, USA Today,The Wall Street Journal,The Washington Examiner, American HunterMagazine, and ABC News.

Giles and his wife Margaret have two daughters, Hannah and Regis. Hannah devastated ACORN with her 2009 nation-shaking undercover videos and she currently stars in the explosive 2018 Tribeca Documentary, *Acorn and The Firestorm*.

Regis has been featured in Elle, American Hunter, and Variety magazines. Regis is also the author of a powerful book titled, *How Not To Be A #Me-Too Victim, But A #WarriorChick*.

Regis and Hannah are both black belts in Gracie/Valente Jiu-Jitsu.

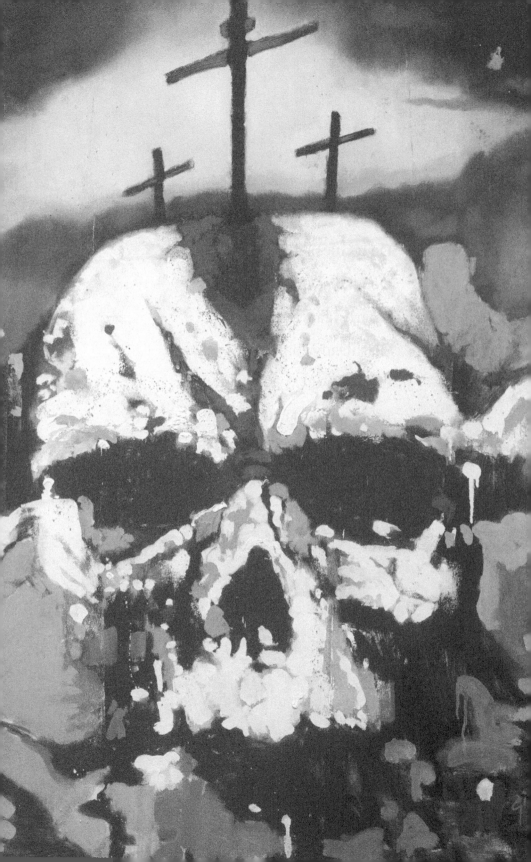

Check out Doug's various websites.

DougGiles.Art

DougGiles.org

SafariCigar.com

ClashDaily.com

ClashNews.US

Instagram @TheGilesWay

Twitter @TheArtOfDoug

# John The Baptist

Accolades for Giles include ...

*"There're those men of the cloth that cater to mediocrity. There are those timid preachers that are straight up cowards, tucking their tails to the truth. Then there's those very few warriors. Doug defines that word. He's a 'Spec-Ops guy' in the Kingdom of God. A true David looking for 'five smooth stones.'*

LTC (Ret.) Pete Chambers Green Beret,
Special Operations Flight Surgeon

*"There is NO way to describe Doug Giles adequately, so I won't even try. Suffice it to say there is NO ONE like him and I'm grateful for him!"*

Eric Metaxas

*"Doug Giles speaks the truth ... he's a societal watchdog ... a funny bastard."*

Ted Nugent

*"Doug Giles is a good man, and his bambinas are fearless. His girls Hannah and Regis Giles are indefatigable. I admire the Giles clan from afar."*

Dennis Miller

*"Doug Giles, the perfect dynamite needed to ignite a fire in the belly of every man, woman and child to live like warriors."*

Lieutenant Colonel Allen B. West

*"Doug is a Wild Man."*

Matt Crouch, President,
Trinity Broadcasting Network

*"Doug Giles brings the heat...as in the exact kind of refining heat the wussified church desperately needs. If you think he is too salty, then bless your heart but stay out of my foxhole because you aren't ready for the battle that has come to the door of the Church. But if you can handle the flames, then get ready to lock shields with Godly warriors called to push back evil at such a time as this. Doug will challenge, inspire, equip, offend, and embolden you...usually all at once and you'll love him for it. Welcome to the fight."*

Rick Green Founder of Patriot Academy

# Doug Giles

Books by Doug Giles

*The Wildman Devotional: A 50 Day Devotional for Men*

*Dear Christian: Your Fear Is Full of Crap*

*Psalms of War: Prayers That Literally Kick Ass*

*The Art of Joe: The Political Brilliance of President Biden*

*Biblical Badasses: The Women*

*If Masculinity is 'Toxic,' Call Jesus Radioactive*

*Would Jesus Vote For Trump?*

*Rules For Radical Christians: 10 Biblical Disciplines for Influential Believers*

*Pussification: The Effeminization Of The American Male*

*Raising Righteous And Rowdy Girls*

*Raising Boys Feminists Will Hate*

*Rise, Kill and Eat: A Theology of Hunting From Genesis to Revelation.*

*If You're Going Through Hell, Keep Going*

*My Grandpa is a Patriotic Badass*

*A Coloring Book for College Cry Babies*

*Sandy Hook Massacre: When Seconds Count, Police Are Minutes Away*

*The Bulldog Attitude: Get It or ... Get Left Behind*

*A Time To Clash*

*10 Habits of Decidedly Defective People: The Successful Loser's Guide to Life*

*Political Twerps, Cultural Jerks, Church Quirks*

Doug's podcast can be seen and heard at
ClashRadio.com.

# John The Baptist

Theologians call these specific prayers from the psalmist David "imprecatory prayers." They are prayers to pull out and pray when things get bad – as in real bad. Prayers you use when a nation's getting mucked up by degenerate priests or politicians, or when the enemy is crushing the people of God, or when your flesh/personal demons are out of control.

King David was the king of this type of incendiary intercession. This giant killer slayed more Goliaths in his prayers and songs than he ever did with a rock and slingshot. Oh, and by the way, Jesus said all those imprecations David dealt out were not the mad ramblings of a ticked off warrior poet, but were actually inspired by the Holy Spirit. (See Matthew 22:43.)

*Psalms of War: Prayers That Literally Kick Ass* is a compendium from the book of Psalms, regarding how David rolled in prayer. I bet you haven't heard these read, prayed, or sung in church against our formidable enemies, have you? I didn't think so. It might be time to dust them off and offer 'em up if you're truly concerned about the state of Christ's Church and our nation.

Also included in this book, *Psalms of War*, are full-color reproductions of the author's original art from his Biblical Badass Series of oil paintings.

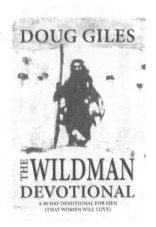

I'm sure some Lysol-disinfected Christian is pearl-clutching over my usage of the word Wildman because they've gotten used to what Satan has sold Christendom namely, a Mild-man. Well, allow me, my fragile friend, to explain what I mean by a biblical Wildman.

Jesus wasn't manageable. He didn't give two flips about what men thought. He wasn't spooked by Satan's threats. He didn't kiss religious or political butt. Jesus was bold, free, and wild before the Father in the epic righteous sense of the word, and you and I should take our cue from the 30-year-old Rebel from Galilee and not castrated Christendom. Can I get a witness?

*The Wildman Devotional: A 50 Day Devotional for Men* will fuel your inner wildman with solid meat from the scripture. In these 200+ pages you'll feast on the wealth, the walk and the warfare of the Christian, that'll prepare you for maximum usefulness this side of the grave. This book is fire!

# John The Baptist

Speaking Engagements

Doug Giles speaks to college, business, community, church, advocacy and men's groups throughout the United States and internationally. His expertise includes issues of Christianity and culture, masculinity vs. wussification, God and government, big game hunting and fishing, raising righteous kids in a rank culture, the Second Amendment, personal empowerment, and social change. To invite Doug to speak at your next event, log on to DougGiles.org and fill out the invitation request.

Made in the USA
Middletown, DE
17 June 2023

32777061R00086